SYMBOLS
of the
HOLY SPIRIT

Symbols of The Holy Spirit

C. Gordon
Brownville

TYNDALE HOUSE PUBLISHERS, INC.
Wheaton, Illinois

Library of Congress Catalog Card Number 78-54038
ISBN 0-8423-6698-9
Copyright © 1978 by Tyndale House Publishers, Inc.,
Wheaton, Illinois.
First printing, September 1978
Printed in the United States of America.

CONTENTS

FOREWORD

Another book on the subject of the Holy Spirit? That reaction would be understandable. In recent years many volumes and articles have been written regarding the third Person of the Trinity.

This book by my friend Gordon Brownville is not a newcomer; it was originally published in 1945. I commend Tyndale House Publishers on reissuing it at this time. Its warmth, scriptural fidelity, and balance give it a timeless appeal and relevance.

In these pages the emphasis is on positive insights to be gained through examination of the various figures of speech employed in the Word of God to describe the ministry of the Spirit of God.

Gordon Brownville is well qualified to write helpfully on this subject. An avid student of Scripture, a respected Bible teacher, and an experienced pastor, he has a deep concern for evangelism and recognizes that the Holy Spirit's presence and power are indispensable in that work. The Billy Graham Evangelistic Association, with which he has ministered, has appreciated his evangelistic passion and spiritual emhasis.

Leighton Ford
Charlotte, North Carolina
March 1978

PREFACE

Those who are conversant with the teachings or even the writings of the Bible know that for instruction the authors have employed the use of things in nature and also various figures of speech. One who reads the Old Testament discovers evidence of this, and of course all who are familiar with the Gospels know that Jesus continually taught by the use of parables. Continuing on into the Epistles, we find Paul and the other apostles often employing the same method of instruction or comparison; and the Book of the Revelation is perhaps the most figurative in speech and language of all the books of the Bible. Various figures of speech and other literary devices are employed, as metaphors, similes, parables, allegories, types, symbols, and emblems. All of these are generically the same and have approximately the same purpose.

Perhaps a general definition of all might be that it is the use of some figure of speech through which, by which, or in which some truth or lesson is seen or taught. In other words, behind every figure there is a reality of truth to be emphasized and remembered. The figure is used for a purpose, and he who would understand the teachings must, through analysis of the figure, discover the reality for which it speaks.

In the thirteenth chapter of Matthew Jesus employs seven parables, often characterized as Kingdom Parables, in which he speaks of a sower, seed, a field, a pearl, the leaven, the tares and wheat, and the dragnet; and it is necessary, if we would understand just what he is teaching, to discover the truth in its relationship to these figures. This can be done by seeking to make oneself acquainted with the figure itself.

For instance, if it be something taken from nature, we must discover everything possible in regard to that particular part of nature: its derivation, its duty, its location, its method of growth, its usefulness to the creation about it and to man. When we have discovered these things, then we have taken the first step toward understanding the reality of truth which the Spirit of God has hidden behind them. We must remember that spiritual things are spiritually discerned, and that for our true instruction there must be the illumination of the Spirit of God, plus that which we have discovered through our study of the natural law in its relationship to the figure used.

It is a fact that thousands, yes millions, in every age do not understand the teachings of the Word of God because the Spirit of God has not become their teacher, and he who knows the mind of God has not had the privilege of revealing it to them. This is why purely secular education can never give spiritual insight into the things that are eternal, and why oftentimes those comparatively ignorant, insofar as any cultural background or training may be concerned, yet have a deeper insight into things of the Spirit than those with great intellectual ability.

My purpose in the following messages is to discover, firstly, those figures of speech through which the Holy Spirit in his Person and ministry is related to Jesus Christ as the Son of man in his great incarnate and redemptive ministry; and, secondly, to discover the ministry of the Holy Spirit in his relationship through Christ to us who have become the sons of God through faith in his Name.

Suffice it to say that everything which shall be set down hereafter is based upon my firm conviction and the scriptural fact that the Spirit of God is the third Person of the Holy Trinity, very God of very God, equal with the Father and with the Son, and coeternal and coexistent. He who does not recognize the deity and personality of the Holy Spirit will find no help or benefit from the following pages. One who denies to him this place can never find blessing through a mere influence or spirit emanating from the fact that God lives, that Christ died, and that through his teachings the world is being permeated with righteousness. There is too much fact to deny this; and, of course, one who does not rely upon the divine personality of the Holy Spirit cannot know his power through impartation and indwelling in his own life. A mere influence can never produce what we shall discover in our various studies.

To me it seems that a misunderstanding of the person and ministry of the Holy Spirit accounts for the majority of vagaries of interpretation and experience always labeled as Christian and often found within the fellowship of the Church, and which when followed to their logical end produce nothing but confusion plus, oftentimes, insanity or rejection of even Christ himself. There are too many evidences all about us to deny this fact; and the only answer is to rightly determine and understand the ministry and purpose of the Holy Spirit to those who believe he has been given from God the Father in answer to the prayer of Jesus Christ on our behalf. Remember, Jesus said that he is "the Spirit of truth."

C. G. B.

LIKE A DOVE 1

*"And Jesus, when he was baptized, went up straight-
way out of the water: and, lo, the heavens were opened
unto him, and he saw the Spirit of God descending like
a dove, and lighting upon him: and lo a voice from
heaven, saying, This is my beloved Son, in whom I am
well pleased."* (Matthew 3:16, 17)

Our first study will consider the ministry of the Holy Spirit not
only as he reveals himself in the form of a dove, but as he produces
in Christ and in those who are Christ's in this age or dispensation
the dovelike qualities of life that have set this creature of God
uniquely apart from all others which wing their way through the
heavens. All of us are acquainted with the dove, and naturalists
tell us that there is very little difference between one variety and
another, whether it be the pure white dove, the homing pigeon, or
any other type. They all have similar characteristics, and our
lesson can be learned from the whole family.

In reading again the account of the baptism of Jesus, we are informed that "the heavens were opened unto him, and he saw the
Spirit of God descending like a dove, and lighting upon him: and
lo a voice from heaven, saying, This is my beloved Son, in whom I
am well pleased." Thus we see that the heavens were opened, sig-
nifying to us that the dove, which was the temporary form in which
the Spirit clothed himself, came directly from the throne of God.
We know this not only because of the opened heavens, but also the

voice of authority as the Father spoke in identifying the One who stood in Jordan as his only begotten Son.

Gathered about John and Jesus as they were standing in the waters of Jordan no doubt were many of the disciples of John; for they had been very much interested in this One of whom John spoke, and, according to the record, soon left John to follow him. Of John himself Jesus said: "Among them that are born of women there hath not risen a greater than John the Baptist" (Matt. 11:11). And yet, in spite of the presence of this great man of whom Jesus said none had ever surpassed him in greatness of life and character, and the others who stood about, the dove descended and lighted upon only one, the Son of man.

There is much similarity between this incident, that is, so far as spiritual comparison is concerned, and the account of Noah's experience when he first opened the windows of the ark. Turning back to Genesis, we read that after the rains had ceased, Noah opened the window of the ark and let the dove loose. She was later to return without finding any place where the waters had abated and where she might rest her tiny feet. But the thing we would suggest here is that Noah was the father of the righteous, for we are told that of all that antediluvian civilization, only Noah was found a righteous man; and he with his sons and their wives were saved from that terrible judgment. As the dove went forth from the hand of Noah, the father of the righteous, so the dove has come forth from the hand of God, who indeed is the righteous Father and the Father of the righteous. We hear him say again, "This is my beloved Son."

The Holy Spirit came in order that he might not only rest upon him, but that he might dwell in him. John, in describing this, writes: "I saw the Spirit descending from heaven like a dove, and it abode upon him. And I knew him not: but he that sent me to baptize with water, the same said unto me, Upon whom thou shalt see the Spirit descending, and remaining on him, the same is he which baptizeth with the Holy Ghost" (John 1:32, 33). He whose body had been conceived by the Holy Spirit and who had performed every act and spoken every word under the complete domination of the Spirit now has the public attestation of this fact.

Like a Dove

There are many who would debate and argue and split theological hairs as to when Jesus became conscious of his divine mission. Personally, and with the Scriptures, there seems to be no reason why such argument should be given. If he is the eternal God, how could he ever be unconscious or unmindful of his eternal state as well as his human ministry? The thing we are interested in here is the descent of the dove from the Father in identification of the Son. Here is the public declaration of the complete indwelling of the Holy Spirit in the Son of man.

Not, as the unscriptural view would maintain, that he had the divine only insofar as all men have a spark of divine. No, he was more than a mere man with a spark of the divine in his breast; he was Son of God and Son of man, the God-Man in a very unique way.

Having identified the Son of man, the Spirit of God now leads him into his ministry; and as we follow along in the Gospel record, he is led of the Spirit into the wilderness for a period and at the close of this experience comes into contact with temptations which beset humanity. In the three temptations recorded, we find that directly or indirectly every root from which human temptations spring was uncovered, and the suggested fruit thereof rejected and set aside. This rejection came because of the enabling power of the Spirit of God within.

Continuing on in Christ's ministry, we discover that he went about doing good, giving sight to the blind, unstopping deaf ears, healing and cleansing the lepers, even raising the dead, as well as making prophetic, spiritual, ethical, and moral pronouncements which have changed in the years, not in content, but in the ever-increasing value and paramount position they hold. Never have his utterances been surpassed or their truths set aside. Even through his death he was empowered by the complete indwelling of the Holy Spirit, and was able to offer himself "through the eternal Spirit . . . without spot to God" (Heb. 9:14), both as a sacrifice and as an atonement for the sin of humanity.

The first evidence in Scripture of the Holy Spirit is given to us in the opening verses of the Book of Genesis: "And the Spirit of God moved upon the face of the waters" (Gen. 1:2). Marsh, in his

17

instructive book,* to which book I am greatly indebted in the preparation of these messages, suggests that the word which our margin gives as "brooded" is translated in the Vulgate by the Latin word *incubabat*, which means incubated, and gives to us the picture of a bird sitting on a nest of eggs and warming them into life.

Is not this the very thing that the Spirit of God did in that fateful day? Chaos and darkness were upon the face of the deep, and the Holy Spirit hovered, or brooded, over this chaotic condition, incubating it by his own regenerating power and bringing it back into life and beauty again. This introduction to the ministry of the Holy Spirit throws great light upon his work and ministry as the third Person of the Holy Trinity. He is the Regenerator, the Incubator, and the Enabler of life.

In his productiveness, the Spirit of God produces, first in Christ and then in those who are united in life in him, dovelikeness. The dovelikeness perhaps is found first of all in the purity of the dove life. Solomon, speaking of his bride, says, "My dove, my undefiled" (Song 5:2). Naturalists tell us that the dove is a clean bird, and we know this to be true from the teaching of Scripture, for the dove described as clean was permissible for sacrifice.

The mother of Jesus, after the days of her purification, went to the Temple "to offer a sacrifice according to that which is said in the law of the Lord, A pair of turtledoves, or two young pigeons" (Luke 2:24). There are, of course, many not of the evangelical persuasion who believe that Mary not only conceived in her womb by the overshadowing of the Holy Ghost, but that her mother in turn so conceived, and that Mary was born immaculate or without sin. We know that this is a dogma of very late date, and that many of the learned Roman Catholic cardinals argued earnestly against the adoption of this doctrine, but in vain; and we also know that no such claim is justified. Indeed it is refuted, as revealed by this act of hers in offering a sacrifice for her own impurity.

Without question, Jesus Christ had the purity of dovelikeness. This purity came through one source, as we have seen, even the indwelling of the Holy Spirit. So certain was he of his purity of life

Emblems of the Holy Spirit.

Like a Dove

that he, as none of us ever can, could stand before his enemies and challenge them, "Which of you convinceth me of sin?" (John 8:46). And to this day, while attempts have been made by pagan philosophers to accuse him of sin and even immorality in prosecuting or perpetuating his message, none has been successful; and even some who have tried to hold such a view have given up in despair, only to throw themselves before him in adoration and worship and recognize that between him and God there is no difference.

Not only did Jesus claim this sinlessness, but the Father recognized and attested the same. Twice the Father spoke from heaven in regard to his Son: once, as we have seen, at the time of baptism, and, secondly, on the Mount of Transfiguration. You will remember that as the three disciples looked up, they saw Jesus transfigured before them: "And behold a voice out of the cloud, which said, This is my beloved Son, in whom I am well pleased; hear ye him" (Matt. 17:5). With Jesus on the Mount were Moses and Elijah, one representing the law, the other representing the prophets. Jesus in his glory, when transfigured, was not in such condition by some external act of the Father, but through his own purity.

In other words, stepping aside momentarily from things earthly, his human perfection shone out in its glory, the glory, at least in part, which our first parents had in the Garden. Moses was there representing the law in order that he might testify to the fact that the law had been completely fulfilled; and here was one Man who was justified by the deeds of the law. Elijah was there representing the prophets; and he could testify that all prophecies concerning this One, insofar as his first advent and his human perfection were concerned, had been absolutely fulfilled.

Thus does he have the divine approbation of his Father in his dovelike purity. But even his enemies attest this fact, for it was Pilate's wife who called him a just man, and Pilate himself found no reason for condemnation. The centurion at the cross, in the moment when the sun refused to shine and the earth shook, declared, "Certainly this was a righteous man" (Luke 23:47). Jesus Christ was in all points pure and dovelike, made possible by the indwelling of the Spirit of purity in himself.

19

Symbols of the Holy Spirit

Perhaps little realized by believers is the truth that as the Holy Spirit has produced dovelike purity in the Son of man, he also is producing it in those who believe. There is a twofold meaning in sanctification, for which the Greek word is *hagios*. The primary meaning is "to set apart"; but the secondary meaning is "to make holy," and it is the work of the Holy Spirit in sanctification that brings to us true holiness. We need to realize this, because much self-effort produces only self-righteousness, and that is "as filthy rags." Paul tells us, "The foundation of God standeth sure, having this seal, The Lord knoweth them that are his. And, Let every one that nameth the name of Christ depart from iniquity" (2 Tim. 2:19). He has quoted from two different passages, one in Numbers and the other in Isaiah; but in doing so, has shown us that what God expects of us is purity of life, and that this is one of the two stones upon which the foundation of God standeth sure.

So much harm has been brought to the cause of Christ by those who have failed to recognize this truth that the damage may never be comprehended short of eternity. Self-righteousness turns people from God and causes one to be a spiritual monstrosity; but righteousness in the Spirit and purity produced by the Spirit place the beauty of Christ upon us, and the beauty of such holiness causes him to say, "My dove, my undefiled." And it causes others to see in us the dovelike purity that was his.

Jesus instructed his disciples that they should be "wise as serpents, and harmless as doves" (Matt. 10:16). The dove here is referred to as a bird that is harmless and when one is harmless, then one must be gentle. It has been suggested that one reason for the gentleness of the dove is that the bird has no liver bile or gall, the gall having been considered by naturalists of old as the source and fount of contention, the bitterness of the gall being supposed to infuse itself into the spirit. The Holy Spirit has no gall and thus can produce in us the gall-less life, or the life that is gentle and kind.

As the ninefold fruit of the Spirit is enumerated for us, we read: "The fruit of the Spirit is ... gentleness" (Gal. 5:22). The Greek word used here is *kristotes* and means kindness that is useful or serviceable; or one might say, not namby-pamby. Recently two of my members were having a discussion, one having found some reason to criticize the other, and the other rightly protesting the criticism. It seems as though a sensitive Christian had become more sensitive and imagined that the brother had not spoken or acted kindly toward him. In the course of the conversation between these two, as this was mentioned the brother accused said something like this: "I'm not going to play nursemaid to any sensitive Christian." As we think about this, we discover that there is a world of common sense and truth and a guide to spiritual conduct wrapped up in the statement.

To show a false kindness and be namby-pamby with such Christians, or as he said, to be "a nursemaid" to them, is not the gentleness which is the fruit of the Spirit, but foolishness and undue coddling. Of course, one should at all times conduct himself with the gentleness of the gentleman Jesus.

The word also means utility; and utility, of course, means service that is useful. Perhaps this can best be understood by reference to the game of baseball or any other sport. Every team has a utility player, who must be able to fit into any position on the field, to fit in at the time needed, and to play that position well. He does this only when it is necessary; and when he does it, he must do it without any concern for himself or complaint that he is a mere substitute and that for him there will not be the plaudits of the crowd. Are we willing to be utility players on the great team of God, where life is the stage or the field and we the players? The Psalmist says, "Thy gentleness hath made me great" (Psa. 18:35). The dovelike gentleness of Jesus Christ made him great, and it will make us great when, in the likeness of him and in the power of the divine Spirit, we also become gentle.

One of the most unusual things about the dove is that it is monogamous and keeps itself true to its one mate. The bride, describing her lover in the Song of Solomon, says: "His eyes are as the eyes of doves by the rivers of waters" (Song 5:12). Naturalists tell us that doves by the riverside keep their eyes fixed upon the swirling stream and in drinking, as Pliny observed, do not erect their necks and lift up their heads, but keeping their eyes fixed upon the water, drink a large draught of it, after the manner of beasts. Is this not a picture of the love of Christ in its dovelikeness, loyalty, and faithfulness, as the Holy Spirit causes him to look upon us with sweet delight, fix his eyes upon us, and never remove them? And we know that this is true when we understand the length and the breadth, the height and depth of that love. David, in lamenting the death of Jonathan, said, "Thy love to me was wonderful, passing the love of women" (2 Sam. 1:26). There is only one love that can surpass the love of woman, and that is the love of Jesus Christ for those who are his own, those who are his eternal inheritance, those who believe on his Name.

But it is not sufficient for us just to know the love of Christ which passeth understanding; it is essential that his love might be manifest in us. As his eyes are fixed on us, so ours should be on him. Our love for Christ should be more constant, and we indeed should be monogamous in our spiritual relationship, with no other gods before him, and our affection centered in him and in him alone. We should be able to say with the one quoted above, "He is altogether lovely." In our "Tremont Temple Songs" we have a hymn, one of the stanzas of which is:

> *Since my eyes were fixed on Jesus,*
> *I've lost sight of all beside;*
> *So enchained my spirit's vision,*
> *Looking at the Crucified.*
>
> *All for Jesus! all for Jesus!*
> *Looking at the Crucified;*
> *All for Jesus! all for Jesus!*
> *Looking at the Crucified.*

Is our love constant and true? It can be such only as the Spirit of God spreads his love abroad in our hearts and makes us like the dove, of one love.

Each of us is ever conscious of the past and the life out of which he has been saved. Oftentimes there come moments of retrogression or of remembrance which cause our cheeks to blush with shame, and we wonder whether the soil of the past has been entirely removed. Wonderful words were recorded by the Psalmist: "Though ye have lain among the pots, yet shall ye be as the wings of a dove covered with silver, and her feathers with yellow gold" (Psa. 68:13). All of us have lain among the pots of sin; and how wonderful to know that as we have ascended from that place of defilement, we have been cleansed with the purifying power of the Spirit of God, and that to us has been given the beauty of the dove life.

I think it is Moulton who, in one of his books dealing with the Holy Land, tells of the flat roofs of the houses in Palestine and the habit of the dove in hiding away during the heat of the day beneath the broken pitchers and rubbish placed there. Broken pitchers were put there perhaps to protect the property by preventing intruders from mounting the stairs to the flat roof and making a forceful entrance into the house. During the last war, when I was stationed in Salisbury Plain, England, I went to the nearby town of Farnum and saw this sort of protection for the first time. On the top of a large cement wall were embedded pieces of broken bottles and broken glass to keep people from climbing over to enter the premises.

We are told that as the shadows begin to lengthen and the sun begins to set, the pigeons suddenly emerge from behind the pitchers and other rubbish, where they had been sleeping in the heat of the day or pecking about to find food, and dart upward, flying in large circles, with their outspread wings catching the bright glow of the sun's diminishing rays. So, as described by the Psalmist, they really appear to have their wings covered with silver, most of these doves being pure white. And as they catch the bright glow of the sun, they seem to have feathers of yellow gold. As they soar away into the heavens, they reveal the beauty of their heaven-given plumage.

Perhaps you have noticed that a dove or pigeon is always in a clean and unsullied condition. Not only does the Holy Spirit bring us this dovelike beauty as we ascend out of the old life of sin and death, but he continues it, keeping us unsullied and unsoiled from our contact with the world, if only we will let him. Unsullied, so that when we come to the time of sunset and lengthening shadows, we will, as spirits justified and cleansed, fly away to be with him; and the beauty of our life will be as though our wings were of silver and our feathers of gold.

As we have discovered, at the baptism of Jesus the dove was a messenger sent out from the Father, and the same intimation is

Symbols of the Holy Spirit

given by the Psalmist: "Oh that I had wings like a dove!" (Psa. 55:6). The dove is a messenger, especially the homing pigeon. In fact, the ability of the dove to return as a messenger to his home from far distant places is one of the marvels of nature. Thus the dove symbolizes to us the Spirit of God as his messenger, bringing first to our hearts the message of eternal peace.

The second time Noah loosed the dove from the window of the ark it returned with an olive leaf in its beak. The olive leaf is the symbol of peace; and Noah knew by this that the waters of judgment had abated and the dry land had appeared. It was only after the waters of baptism had fallen from the body of Jesus as he rose from the watery grave that the Spirit descended as the messenger upon him who is the Prince of Peace. In him, as symbolized by his coming forth from the waters in Jordan, the waters of judgment have abated for all who will believe.

As John describes the descent of the Spirit in the form of a dove, he distinctly says that the Spirit is to remain as an abiding presence in Christ. Referring back to the experience of Noah, we remember that when the window of the ark was opened for the third time and the dove sent forth, it did not return but went to its abiding place on the cleansed earth. Thus the Holy Spirit did not go back into heaven, but abode in Jesus in all his fullness. This fullness of the Spirit was his not only at all times in the Incarnation, but eternally; we cannot divide the Trinity or the Godhead. But here it is manifest, that we might believe and understand.

No greater truth can be discovered by the believer in this dispensation than that which Jesus clearly taught: "I will pray the Father, and he shall give you another Comforter [Paraclete], that he may abide with you for ever; even the Spirit of truth; whom the world cannot receive, because it seeth him not, neither knoweth him: but ye know him; for he dwelleth with you, and shall be in you" (John 14:16, 17). Out of this promise of the Lord let us remember the expressions that deal with the time of the Spirit's abiding—"with you for ever," and "dwelleth with you, and shall be in you."

Many sincere Christians feel that by their failures they drive the Spirit away, but if Jesus' words are true, this is an utter impossibility. It is true that he may dwell in our hearts as our new life in

24

Like a Dove

Christ, thus making us partakers of his divine nature; but he may not occupy all phases of our life. There is a difference between his permanent dwelling in us from the moment of regeneration and his occupying us in all his fullness.

We have received him in his fullness, for he is a divine person and cannot give himself in part, but must come in whole. But the question is, Has he been allowed by us to occupy every phase of our life, every vessel in our body, that not only dwelling in us but remaining with us, he might indeed fill us with his own presence?

Thus have we sought to reveal, both by the help of others and our own research, to understand the ministry of the Holy Spirit through his likeness to a dove. There are other realms of comparison that might be made, but perhaps the foregoing will not only illuminate and instruct the believer in the ways of the Spirit, but also be an incentive to more complete study and thus result in the reception of greater revelation through the Spirit of God. One delight in our study of the Word is that it is exhaustless and always presenting some new realm of truth and its application.

When the great Norwegian explorer Roald Amundsen, who was the first to discover the magnetic meridian of the North Pole and to discover the South Pole, and the first and only one to fly over the North Pole in a lighter-than-air machine, made one of his trips into the North, he took one of his homing pigeons along with him. When he had reached his destination, he opened its cage and set it free. Imagine the delight of his wife, back in Norway, when she looked up from the doorway of her home and saw the pigeon circling about in the sky above. Is it any wonder she exclaimed, "He is alive"? So when Jesus ascended, the Holy Spirit was given and the disciples could cry, "He is alive." The Spirit of God as a dove has become the messenger to us of the Christ who died but is risen.

THE OIL OF THE   2
DIVINE APOTHECARY

*"And thou shalt speak unto the children of Israel,
saying, This shall be an holy anointing oil unto me
throughout your generations."* (Exodus 30:31)

Oil in the Old and New Testaments symbolizes the Holy Spirit.
For example, in the parable of the virgins the state of unprepared-
ness of the five foolish virgins was evident in their lack of oil. In
other words, they were professors, having the same outward
appearance as the others; but they were not possessors of the
Spirit. It is utterly impossible for one to be fully prepared and
justifiably a professing Christian until he possesses the divine
nature, given through the regenerating powers of the Spirit of
God. The oil which was used for the lamps in the Old Testament,
and for the lamps of the virgins, typifies the oil of the Spirit in
which the light and life of Christ are given to the believer.

When we come to the holy anointing oil, we find this to be different from the other types of oil spoken of in the Word, and the
formula is given by God himself as the Divine Apothecary. The
elements demanded in this formula were of the most costly spices,
and of course this intimates that this oil was more precious than
any other that had been made and, if we are justified in ranking
the ministries of the Holy Spirit, typifies the preciousness of his
highest ministry. As we progress with our thought, we shall come
to a better understanding of this relationship.

26

The Oil of the Divine Apothecary

God is many things, from Creator to Redeemer; but here we find him in the position of the Divine Apothecary, for we read: "After the art of the apothecary . . ." (Exod. 30:25). Surely, such reference and such meticulous care in giving the formula justifies our so defining him. The *American Standard Version* translates this verse as follows: "Compounded after the art of the perfumer." When I was in Cairo just before World War II, I visited the old bazaars, among them a perfume shop. Here were all the various types of oil perfume manufactured in that land. There was "The Secret of the Desert," "The Lotus Flower," and many others. The salesman would open the vial and with a glass applicator apply some to the hand, and then quickly rubbing his hand over it, cause the sweet perfume to diffuse into the air. In the blending of all the perfumes, one realized that they were compounded after the art of the perfumer and by very careful preparation.

We, as believers, need to tarry in the halls of our Divine Perfumer, that we may find our lives sweetened by the rich perfume of his Spirit. You will recall Queen Esther and her days of preparation. One year was devoted to this, in order that she might be the most exquisite and beautiful maiden the king had ever seen. The first six months the perfumers used the oil of myrrh, and then the last six months other perfumes. Is it any wonder that Ahasuerus fell in love with Esther the moment his eyes fell upon her? For "the maiden pleased him" (Esth. 2:9).

So we should be pleasing to King Jesus, and the Holy Spirit is seeking to perfume our lives as with the holy anointing oil, that this might be true. The holy anointing oil used by the priests must have been of the sweetest and richest perfumes, or else God would not so carefully have given the formula and demanded that it be accurately followed.

Analyzing the Oil of Anointing

As God called Moses into his laboratory and told him how to make this oil, so I believe we should enter into the laboratory of the Scriptures, discovering the full meaning of the various component elements we use, that the spiritual implication or revelation of these things in the ministry of the Holy Spirit may be made known to us and effective in us, that our lives may be the very perfume of his presence.

Once again let us remind ourselves that this is not the oil that was used for the lamps which lighted the Tabernacle or the Temple. This was distinctly called a holy anointing oil, as we have seen, made by a divine formula. A warning needs to be given here, lest perhaps someone attempt to apply the work of the Holy Spirit to the unregenerate and carnal heart. God distinctly says, "Upon man's flesh shall it not be poured, neither shall ye make any other like it, after the composition of it: it is holy, and it shall be holy unto you" (Exod. 30:32). Is not this a very definite warning that an unregenerate nature cannot be reformed?

The holy anointing oil was not to be placed upon man's flesh, but only upon the one qualified to be so anointed. Man's nature is sinful. Paul said, "I know that in me (that is, in my flesh), dwelleth no good thing" (Rom. 7:18). God does not try to reform, nor to pour the oil of his Spirit upon the old nature. He creates anew. "If any man be in Christ, he is a new creature: old things are passed away" (2 Cor. 5:17). And we know that this new creation is possible only by the regenerating work of the Holy Spirit. Let us be guarded, then, lest we attempt to apply the Spirit's ministry to those who have not been born again. We find also that no imitations were to be made. "Neither shall ye make any other like it, after the composition of it."

So many today are following substitutes and imitations, but are getting none of the Spirit himself. Oh, that men would see that only that which qualifies itself within the formula of God can be the genuine! As in all days, people today are suffering under false delusions and seem not to be able to discern the mind or the Person of the Spirit. As we will show later on, it was impossible for the formula to be fulfilled and the oil given, which was its main ingredient, until the olive had been crushed. So also there cannot be a transformation of nature without co-crucifixion by faith with and in Jesus Christ.

Now let us proceed to the analysis of the ingredients. Reading the Scripture, you will note that God said, "Take thou also unto thee principal spices" (Exod. 30:23). The word "principal" literally means "excellent, or nothing inferior." How true this is

The Oil of the Divine Apothecary

of the Holy Spirit! He gives only the best, and produces but the best in his gifts.

This is taught in the story of Abraham who, in order that he might find a maiden who would be the bride for his son Isaac, sent the faithful servant Eleazar back into the country from which he had come. In this account we discover that Eleazar, having found the maiden, immediately proceeded to shower her with rich and beautiful gifts. Is not this what the Holy Spirit, who seeks a bride for Jesus Christ in a strange country, is doing as the Servant of God the Father? He is showering God's best gifts upon us, which is one of his most important ministries.

The first ingredient was the "pure myrrh." It is interesting to discover its source. We find that myrrh comes from a small tree in Arabia. This tree has odoriferous wood and bark. The myrrh was obtained in two ways, either by making an incision and allowing the sap or oil to run out, I suppose very much in the same way that trees in the Southland are tapped for turpentine, or from the gum which exudes from the bark of the tree, as the sap exudes from our spruce gum. The myrrh obtained by the latter method was called pure myrrh because of its purity and because it flowed freely or without the act of man. In fact, the *American Standard Version* translates the words "pure myrrh" as "flowing myrrh." Rotherham translates it "self-flowing myrrh."

Thus we see the source from which this pure myrrh is obtained as it flows without the hand of man from the bark of the tree. Just so is the Holy Spirit altogether pure and self-giving. There is no need for any self-incision or tempting of the Spirit in his coming. Only as he flows naturally from within can he produce in us the pure myrrh of his blessings.

Now we should determine the uses to which pure myrrh was put. Scripture references must be studied to understand and make comparison. "All thy garments smell of myrrh" (Psa. 45:8). There is no doubt that this is messianic, and that the Psalmist is speaking of Jesus Christ, the divine Messiah. In Proverbs 7:17 we read, "I have perfumed my bed with myrrh." This is a description of the arts and devices of a wicked woman seeking to lure men to their destruction. But has she not stolen that which is beautiful from those who are not wicked, but pure? Every child will remember the beautiful scent of his mother's handkerchief box. Every man who has ever carried on a correspondence with a lady with whom he is in love can never forget the rich perfumes which escaped from her envelope the moment it was opened.

Myrrh was used for its rich fragrance, and so illustrates how the Holy Spirit seeks to make fragrant this life of ours, that it can be said of us, "All thy garments smell of myrrh." Then again, myrrh was used for purification, as we discover in the account of Esther in her twelve months of purification and beautification that she might find favor with the king. Six months' application of pure myrrh was used in this purification. In this we see that the Holy Spirit has anointed us with pure myrrh, not only for fragrance, but also that he might make us pure. Not the purity of self-effort, but the purity of a progressive sanctification, made beautiful because he himself is the Purifier. It is utterly impossible for us to have in our lives the results of such purification without him. All else is but productive of self-righteousness and ultimate dismay.

Myrrh was used also as a sort of anesthetic or deadener of pain. Mark records that "they gave him to drink wine mingled with myrrh: but he received it not" (Mark 15:23). Jesus, as he hung there upon the Cross, was not seeking any softening or deadening of pain. It was often mingled with wine, in adulteration, and in this form it was offered to him as an escape from pain and suffering. And because his ministry was unique and he must go to the ultimate of human suffering, it was, of course, refused. Neither will the Holy Spirit be given to us to act as some escape from pain or suffering; but with the myrrh, he will comfort and deaden spiritual pains and ease the heartache. This the Spirit of God continually does for all who trust in him. Thus we see that the first ingredient in the holy anointing oil reveals the Spirit's work of producing the perfume of God's sweetness upon our life, the purity of the Spirit of God in our life, and the easing of the pains and heartaches along life's pathway.

The second ingredient was the "sweet cinnamon," which was derived from the aromatic inner rind or bark of the *laurus cinnamon*, a small evergreen tree, which is mentioned only three times in the Old Testament. In the Song of Solomon, he compares the bride to "a garden inclosed" (Song 4:12), and enumerates cinnamon among the things found there. Perhaps this was a tree which had been brought for the king's garden from far-off Ceylon, where the choicest of these evergreens grow. Thus the sweet cinnamon of the Spirit of God comes to us in the enclosed garden of our life by the perennial or evergreen consistency, constancy, and undiminishing power of the Holy Spirit.

By a little research we discover that cinnamon has a highly fragrant odor and a peculiarly sweet, warm, and pleasing aromatic taste. Its flavor is due to the aromatic oil. This is prepared by pounding the bark and lacerating it in seawater, and then quickly distilling the whole. Is not this illustrative of the working of the Holy Spirit as he anoints us, that as cinnamon we might be sweetened in life, that our innermost being might be tempered with the grace of patience and forbearance, and that we should be of a peculiarly sweet, warm, and pleasing aromatic taste to those with whom we come in contact?

To understand, to be sympathetic, and not to be unkind and rash. This is the fruit of the Spirit, and ought to be found more often in the lives of those who profess the most. Marsh quotes Charles Swain as saying of good temper, it is:

> *A charm to banish grief away,*
> *To free the brow from care—*
> *Turns tears to smiles, makes dullness gay,*
> *Spreads gladness everywhere.*

Thus, this second ingredient in the divine formula for the holy anointing oil brings to us a revelation of the Spirit's ministry as he produces through the broken body of the Lord a strange, pleasing flavor and a peculiarly fragrant odor in our lives.

The third ingredient is "sweet calamus," the pith of a scented cane probably found in western Asia Minor. It was very fragrant when bruised. It was the inner portion that brought forth the fragrance. This seems to me emblematic of the Holy Spirit as he produces in us his internal thoughts, feelings, and affections, as he brings to us the solitude of inner grace. According to Isaiah 43:24, sweet calamus was used in sacrifice: "Thou hast bought me no sweet cane with money, neither hast thou filled me with the fat

31

of thy sacrifices: but thou hast made me to serve with thy sins, thou hast wearied me with thine iniquities." The word that is used here for sweet cane is the same as the sweet calamus.

To every Christian there come moments of solitude and aloneness in which we hear the voice of the Spirit speaking softly to our souls. Perhaps in words expressed so beautifully in the following lines:

> *Be still my soul,*
>   *Thy Father loveth thee;*
> *Fret not, nor murmur*
>   *At thy weary lot;*
> *Though dark and lone*
>   *Thy journey seem to be,*
> *Be sure that thou*
>   *Art ne'er by him forgot.*
> *He ever loves; then trust him,*
>   *Trust him still;*
> *Let all thy care be this—*
>   *The doing of his will.*
> *Canst thou not trust*
>   *His rich and bounteous hand*
> *Who feeds all living things*
>   *On sea and land?*
> *Be thou content.*

The fourth ingredient in the divine formula was "cassia." In the *American Standard Version*, the margin gives it as "costus," and we discover that it probably was the costus of the ancients, a composite plant with purple flowers, discovered by one Falcone. It grows in Cashmere at a height of about 8,000–9,000 feet above sea level. It is exported to various countries, and its value is found primarily in its roots. How suggestive this is of the Spirit's ministry in us!

The costus has a purple flower, and is this not suggestive of the fact that, as purple is the color of royalty, so the Spirit of God gives to us the nobility of heaven! Born of the Spirit into the family of God, we become of royal lineage and family. Then we discover that it grows at a height of from 8,000–9,000 feet above

The Oil of the Divine Apothecary

sea level, and this to me is most suggestive, for the Holy Spirit has caused us to be lifted up in Christ and to sit in the heavenlies with him. Possessors of resurrection life in the Spirit, we are privileged to be in the heavenlies with him, far above the polluted atmosphere of this natural life. Living above while living below! This is made possible only through the indwelling and uplifting power of the Spirit of God.

Recall that the chief virtue of the plant is found in its roots, in which the commercial value is found. Once again, this reminds us of the workings of the Spirit in that he is the One who roots, or grounds, and establishes us in Jesus Christ. Only through him and his divine teaching can any of us cause our roots to grow deeper into the soil of things eternal. To be rooted in him is to be of spiritual value.

The last ingredient, and the one which was the foundation for the others, was olive oil. This, we know, is obtained by crushing the fleshy part of the olive. How symbolic this is of the giving of the Holy Spirit through the crushing or bruising of the Heavenly One. Not until Jesus Christ had been glorified—and he could not be glorified until he was crucified—could the oil of the Holy Spirit be given.

Thus the oil of the Spirit has become the base or foundation for all of our blessings in Christ. Surely, when God gave the divine formula, naming the ingredients, he chose them not only because of their costliness and fragrance and purifying powers, but also because they would be so symbolic and typical and emblematic of himself in the Person and ministry of his Holy Spirit.

The Men Anointed

Turning back to the Scriptures, we read, "And thou shalt anoint Aaron and his sons, and consecrate them, that they may minister unto me in the priest's office" (Exod. 30:30). Aaron, the High Priest of Israel, and his sons were to be consecrated for this office by anointing them with the holy anointing oil. But Scripture teaches that Aaron is but a type of another. In the Epistle to the Hebrews we find the comparison between the Aaronic priesthood and the priesthood of Jesus Christ. As Moses anointed Aaron with

Symbols of the Holy Spirit

the holy anointing oil, so "God anointed Jesus of Nazareth" (Acts 10:38). He is our Greater Priest, the One who has fulfilled the priesthood in Aaron and upon whom, in consecrating him to this heavenly calling, the holy anointing oil of the Spirit has been placed.

But there is a lesser priesthood, for there were the sons of Aaron, and so there are the sons of God, those who through faith in Jesus Christ have entered into this eternal relationship. As the sons of Aaron were anointed with the holy anointing oil, so the sons of God in Christ have been anointed, for the Word declares: "He which... hath anointed us, is God" (2 Cor. 1:21). Every born-again individual has been anointed with the Holy Spirit by God the Father, even as the sons of Aaron were anointed with the holy anointing oil. This is our priesthood.

The Vessels Anointed

Turning again to the Scriptures describing the holy anointing oil, we discover that the vessels of the Tabernacle were to be anointed with the oil. These vessels are enumerated for us. Typically, they are all types of Jesus Christ, either in his Person or in his ministry. God tabernacled in the midst of Israel in the Tent of Meeting and revealed his glory in the holiest place of all. But today he has tabernacled himself in Jesus Christ his Son, and through him in us. Paul tells us that "your body is the temple of the Holy Ghost which is in you" (1 Cor. 6:19). The word used here for temple is one of two Greek words, meaning "the holiest place of all." The other which is used in the New Testament means the entire Temple area.

Thus we see that as the Tabernacle was anointed, typical of the anointing of Jesus Christ in whom God the Father was tabernacled during the Incarnation, so our body has been; for we are his earthly temple today. How careful we should be, lest we desecrate this sacred place!

Not only was the Tabernacle itself anointed with the holy anointing oil, but the Ark of the Covenant, which was placed in the holiest place. This was where God dwelt, where he manifested his *shekinah* glory, and is suggestive of the place where God dwells in us, out of which he shows his *shekinah* glory and speaks. The heart is the center of affection, for "out of it are the issues of life" (Prov. 4:23). As the heart and life of Jesus Christ were anointed, so also our hearts have been anointed with the Holy Spirit or the holy anointing oil, that that which issues forth therefrom might be to the glory of his name.

We have already mentioned the vessels that were found in the holiest place, but perhaps a brief enumeration of them, with their suggestiveness, will be helpful. There was the table, on which could be found the shewbread. Paul said, "When it pleased God, who separated me from my mother's womb, and called me by his grace, to reveal his Son in me ... I conferred not with flesh and blood" (Gal. 1:15, 16). When he refers to God revealing his Son in him, he is literally saying that God is making a show thing out of him for his Son. Our life must be as shewbread on the table, in which God reveals himself. We are anointed of the Spirit that this might be true.

Then there was the seven-branched golden candlestick, representative of the nation Israel and the light that was to shine through them. The light was kept burning by the supply of oil. This candlestick was anointed with the holy anointing oil, because it was a sacred vessel in the Tabernacle of God. In the first chapter of the Revelation we find the description, not of a seven-branch golden candlestick, but of seven individual candlesticks, each one resting upon its own foundation. This teaches us that God does not look upon us as a nation, but as individuals who have come into a personal relationship with him through faith in Jesus Christ.

In other words, each of us is a light-bearer now. Jesus said, "Let your light so shine before men, that they may see your good works, and glorify your Father which is in heaven" (Matt. 5:16). We have been anointed with the holy anointing oil of God's Spirit that we might be as shining lights. This is the Christian dispensation. This is the age of individual grace, blessing, and duty.

Also in this holy place was found the bowl of incense, which continually sent forth its sweet fragrance. In Revelation 5:8 we read, concerning the throne of the Lamb: "The four beasts [living creatures] and four and twenty elders fell down before the Lamb, having every one of them harps, and golden vials full of odors [incense], which are the prayers of saints." That God is pleased when his people pray goes without question; but here is the suggestion that our prayer life should be as a bowl of incense. This prayer life is made possible only through the anointing of the Holy Spirit. Fragrance in prayer life will come when "the Spirit himself maketh intercession for us with groanings which cannot be uttered" (Rom. 8:26). And this is the promise of his ministry. The very perfectness of the prayer life of Jesus may be ours in the power and presence of the Spirit of God.

Outside the Tent of Meeting, but in the confines of the Tabernacle area, was found the altar of sacrifice upon which the offering was made. This too was to be anointed with the holy anointing oil, for this is typical of Christ in his sacrifice for us. We are told that he "through the eternal Spirit offered himself" (Heb. 9:14). This offering was as a sacrifice, for "he was wounded for our transgressions" (Isa. 53:5), and in this sacrifice he made atonement for the sins of the human race. The altar of sacrifice was typical of the Cross, upon which he died and upon which his sacrifice was made. Not necessarily the Cross itself, but the Christ of the Cross. Just so, believers have been anointed with the Spirit that their life might be one of sacrifice and self-abnegation, and that we might fill up those things that remain of the sufferings of Christ. Only as the Spirit of God dwells in us and anoints us can such sacrificial life-giving be attained.

Turning back to the Scriptures, we consider the divine formula or prescription which God the Heavenly Apothecary has given. By blending these ingredients the precious anointing oil was made, and in this blending we discover the gracious ministry of the Holy Spirit in our life. The prayer of our heart ought to be, "Lord, anoint me anew."

I remember when I was a child, my mother had a little hand-painted china bowl. This had two tops, one that fitted over the outside neck of the bottle and one that fitted on the inside. When the first of these was removed and the inner top lifted out, there came the sweet fragrance of attar of roses. For in the bowl were rose petals which had been resting there in darkness for many years. I have read that those who gather the roses from which the perfume is made must work in the depths of night, for the greatest

The Oil of the Divine Apothecary

fragrance of the rose is found in the darkest hour of the night. It is claimed that a rose in sunlight loses approximately 40 percent of its fragrance. During all these years these petals had kept their sweet fragrance, they had been in darkness and crushed.

So we, without the crushing and gloomy sorrow of the years, cannot have the delightful fragrance of the Spirit. Perhaps you have placed a violet or a rose in the leaves of a book and forgotten that you had done this. Then sometime by mere chance the book was opened and the fragrance of the rose came forth. One tells of sending a bunch of violets 7,000 miles, from the Pacific Coast across the United States and across the Atlantic Ocean to faraway England. Nearly a year after, the one to whom they had been sent told his friend, "I have kept those violets in my handkerchief box, and they still shed forth their fragrance." Thus the things which were touched by the rose and the violets were made, like themselves, sweet and fragrant; and so will the oil of the Spirit by his holiness permeate and sweeten in his grace the life of the believer.

Discover the anointing of this holy oil. It is the bestowal of God upon every believer. Its reality ought to be in the experience of each.

THE DEW OF HEAVEN 3

"Israel then shall dwell in safety alone: the fountain of Jacob shall be upon a land of corn and wine; also his heavens shall drop down dew." (Deuteronomy 33:28)

This text will be recognized as part of Moses' farewell to the tribes of Israel. Another had been chosen in his place, and with full knowledge that he was soon to be called into the presence of God, he pronounced his benediction upon the people. That the promise has been completely fulfilled is hard to believe, and those who recognize the prophetic element in this statement believe that in its completeness it will be fulfilled in a later day. However, Moses was speaking, not only of the far-distant future, but of that immediate day and the experience into which Israel soon was to enter. And in that day "the fountain of Jacob will be upon a land of corn and wine; also his heavens shall drop down dew."

The gracious ministry of the Spirit of God in his relationship to Israel was no doubt in the mind of Moses as he made this promise. None other than the Spirit of God, as he empowered the angel of the Lord in that night of wrestling with Jacob, could bring such blessing. Going back to that scene at Jabbok, we see that it is Jacob the Supplanter who after a night of physical and spiritual combat becomes Israel, a prince with God. In the day when this same Jacob stole the blessing rightfully belonging to his brother Esau, his father Isaac in the blessing said, "God give thee of the dew of heaven" (Gen. 27:28). The dews of the Spirit never rested upon the brow of this man until the morning dawned after that eventful night.

It would seem to us that in some degree this is at least suggestive of the position which the Christian or believer in this dispensation holds in his relationship to the Holy Spirit. Those who know of the Spirit's ministry in Old Testament days recognize that it was more or less transient and for specific purposes. In contrast with this, we know that at Pentecost he was given in all his fullness, and has been since to those who believe.

Through the nation Israel, the promise had been given of a new heart and a new spirit, which no doubt clearly refers to the gift of the Holy Spirit in his fullness, if Israel had been willing to receive. However, with the rejection of Jesus Christ, God's Son, this privilege was set aside, and the Christian becomes the recipient of the blessing. At least it would seem permissible to draw this conclusion from the experience of Jacob in receiving the blessing from his father. God has given us the "dew of heaven."

For our instruction, it will be necessary to acquaint ourselves with the natural law in its relationship to dew. We should know the hygrometrics of dew, and also the law of physics by which it is explained. The dictionary tells us that "dew is moisture deposited in minute drops upon any cool surface by condensation of the vapor of the atmosphere, formed after a hot day during or toward night, and plentiful in the early morning; and in the form of ice it is called hoarfrost." All of us have seen the dew on the grass on such a morning, but perhaps have not stopped to consider the natural law which explains to us how it came to be there.

Before we become amateur physicists, it might be interesting to study the dew from the scriptural standpoint. For instance, many Bible expositors believe that there was no rain upon the earth in the antediluvian days, and that Genesis 2:5, 6, "The Lord God had not caused it to rain upon the earth . . . but there went up a mist from the earth, and watered the whole face of the ground," definitely teaches that until the Flood, God had caused the earth to be watered by exceptionally heavy dew. Perhaps up to this time the nights were clear and the days practically cloudless, so that this phenomenon could be produced. In reading the account of the Flood, it would seem to suggest that the rainbow was a new phenomenon to Noah, there having been no rainbow until this time. Thus it had singular meaning for him. Even in tropical countries today, as we shall see later, much of the moisture that is given to vegetation comes, not through rain, but from dew.

Of course, dew in the Bible refers to the dews of Palestine or at least the surrounding country. We are told that the dew to which we are accustomed is not the same as that which appears in the East. There is no dew, as we know it, in Palestine; for there is no moisture in the hot summer air to be chilled into dewdrops by the coolness of the night, as in a climate like ours. From May to October, rain is unknown in Palestine, and the sun shines with unclouded brightness day after day. The heat becomes intense during the day, and the ground naturally becomes baked and hardened. Because of this condition vegetation would perish but for the moist west winds that come each night from the waters of the Mediterranean. The bright skies cause the heat to radiate rapidly into space, so that the nights are as cold as the days are hot.

It is to this night coldness that the necessary watering of all plant life is due. The winds coming from the sea are naturally loaded with moisture and as they pass over the earth, which is radiating its heat, the cold air condenses its moisture into drops of water, which fall in a gracious and copious rain of mist on every bit of vegetation. As we shall see later, this differs from the way in which nature produces dew in our own land and with which we are familiar. However, the results are the same in both instances.

Now we shall come to the law of physics as it relates itself to the dew and the hygrometrics of dew, seeking to discover the natural law in regard to these things. Charles Wells, physician at St. Thomas's Hospital, London, in 1814 wrote a thesis entitled, "Essay On Dew," in which he made it clear that the deposit of dew could be satisfactorily explained by the cooling of exposed objects on clear nights; and his theory of automatic cooling by radiation has found a place in all textbooks of physics. The process, as presented by Wells, is simple: All bodies which are at a higher temperature than their surroundings are constantly radiating heat, and cool unless they receive a corresponding amount of heat from other bodies. It requires no elaborate experi-

The Dew of Heaven

ment to show that some bodies radiate more rapidly than others. All nature testifies to this, every still, cloudless summer night.

During the day, objects on the earth's surface gain more heat by radiation than they lose, but as soon as the sun has set this is reversed. Then everything begins to cool by radiation into space. When objects become cool, the air in contact with them becomes chilled. Its watery vapor condenses and collects in tiny liquid drops on their surface. But these dewdrops collect much more abundantly on certain things, such as grass and leaves, than on others, such as stones and earth. By actual test it has been proven that good radiators are objects that have a dark, roughened, or tarnished surface. These absorb and radiate more quickly than polished and bright surfaces. Every physicist knows the meaning of the dew point, the temperature where the object in its cooling causes the vapor or dew to appear on its surface.

There is a suggestiveness in the discovery that the rough and tarnished surfaces make the best radiators. All of us have been redeemed from a life and nature of sin; eradication has not taken place, but the Spirit of God comes upon us and in us, and finds that that which has been redeemed may become a good radiating surface. Thus we have suggested the physics and hygrometrics of dew from the natural standpoint and also from the scriptural.

We shall now continue to study dew as a revelation of the Holy Spirit and his Person and ministry. "Dewdrops, Nature's tears which she sheds in her own breast for the fair which die. The sun insists on gladness; but at night when he is gone, poor Nature loves to weep." Thus Bailey in *Festus* has described the dew. As the dewdrop is described as Nature's tears of love for those who wilt in the night, so the Spirit of God comes with the dew in the morning as the gift of God, the restorer of the soul, and the satisfier of the heart.

We are told that there are over 31,000 promises in the Bible, but an analysis of these will reveal that there is only one which is distinctly called "the promise of the Father." As Jesus stood on the Mount of Olives with his disciples, he said: "Behold, I send the promise of my Father upon you: but tarry ye in the city of Jerusalem, until ye be endued with power from on high" (Luke 24:49). In the Epistles we read of "that Holy Spirit of promise" (Eph.

Symbols of the Holy Spirit

1:13). The Holy Spirit is God's unique gift to his own in this age. When Isaac pronounced his blessing upon the supplanter Jacob, he said, "God give thee of the dew of heaven" (Gen. 27:28). As the dew is given from heaven, so the Holy Spirit is the direct gift of the Father above to us who were supplanters.

The physicist tells us that the dew comes during the night and is found in the morning. It was after the night of despair, when the disciples waited for the promise of the Father, and in the morning of Pentecost that the Holy Spirit was given in his fullness. And so is the Holy Spirit given to each one who believes, after the dark night of sin and unbelief, on the morning of regeneration. "God . . . hath also given unto us his Holy Spirit" (1 Thess. 4:8).

As each drop of dew is whole and perfect and complete in itself, so the Holy Spirit is given to us in his completeness. "Stars of morning, dewdrops which the sun impearls on every leaf and flower" (Milton). "Every dewdrop and raindrop had a whole heaven within it" (Longfellow, in "Hyperion").

There are many who do not realize the truth of the Holy Spirit's coming in his wholeness, because they have not experienced his complete filling. We must remember that as he is a personality, he cannot come in part. To substantiate this further, reference is made to the Greek word which Jesus used when he gave the promise of "another Paraclete." There are two Greek words meaning "another"; one is the word *heteros*, which means another of a different kind and from which we get our word "heterodoxy"; and the other is *allos*, which means another of the same kind, but one distinct in person. It is this latter word that Jesus used when he gave the promise to his disciples. It is one thing to be fully yielded to the Holy Spirit, that he who indwells us in his fullness may completely fill us; and another thing simply to be indwelt by him when we have not yielded our members to him. When God gave the Holy Spirit to us, he gave him in his entirety. As every dewdrop is a complete world within itself, so to each of us the Holy Spirit is all.

One of the most quoted verses of the Psalms and most picturesque is that which we find in Psalm 133:3—"As the dew of Hermon, and as the dew that descended upon the mountains of Zion" (Psa. 133:3). The Psalmist is speaking of the precious anointing

42

The Dew of Heaven

oil with which Aaron was anointed and of how that oil flowed down from his beard. Then he turns to the picture of Mount Hermon and makes reference to the dew that descends upon the mountains of Zion, not Mount Zion at Jerusalem, but Hermon.

Canon Tristam tells us of the copiousness or plenteousness of the dew of Hermon, and shows how the description given by the Psalmist is exact even to this day. Hermon is a mountain starting from a platform scarcely higher than sea level and rising abruptly to a height of 10,000 feet. At the base of the mountains are found the Upper Jordan Valley and the marshes of Merol. These marshes are for the most part an impenetrable swamp of unknown depth, from which an almost continuous vapor rises under the terrific heat of the rays of the sun. This vapor ascends into the upper atmosphere during the day, comes in contact with the snowy sides of the mountains, and is rapidly congealed and so precipitated in the evening in the form of dew. This dew is so copious that it is almost like rain.

How remarkably this explains the reference made by the Psalmist, and as we consider the dew in its emblematical revelation of the Holy Spirit, we discover that the Holy Spirit is given to us in an inexhaustible supply. At the foot of Hermon beautiful orchards and gardens are to be found—marvelous fertility in a land of almost continuous drought. How else can this be accounted for than by the dew which Nature supplies and which makes possible this magnificent fertility? As the supply of dew is never exhausted from the side of Hermon, so the supply of God's Spirit is inexhaustible, and we draw from a perennial fountain. In fact, the more we draw upon this supply, the more inexhaustible becomes the source. Let no one disparage the grace of God in the gift of his Holy Spirit by saying that he has not given all of himself, or that there is more for him to give. The supply is copious, when we are willing to give back to him in full obedience the vessel in which he dwells, that he may fill it to overflowing.

The ministry of the Holy Spirit restores the soul as the dew restores the soil. Solomon says: "The king's . . . favor is as dew upon the grass" (Prov. 19:12). The word translated "favor" literally means "delight," and is used in Psalm 40:8—"I delight to do thy will, O my God." Our restoration is his delight, for we are told by the Apostle that "we are his workmanship, created in Christ Jesus" (Eph. 2:10). We have been created in Christ Jesus by God's workmanship through the regenerating powers of the Spirit of God, and our soul and life have been restored by him. The word which is translated "workmanship" is the Greek Word *poiema* from the root *poieo*, which means "to make." Therefore, we are God-made. The word *poiema* also gives us our English word "poem," and a poem is defined as "a product of the art of poetry; a concrete expression of feeling and imagination in verse, beautiful, harmonious, and illuminating."

In our restoration we have become God's poem, God's harmony or symphony in Christ, by which in the symmetry and poetic meter of the Spirit of God we have become a concrete expression of his beauty. It is his delight to take the broken vessel of human life and by the touch of the Master hand transform it into such a poem.

Not only does the broken vessel of life, by the touch of the Master's hand, show forth harmony and beauty, but it is ever new. Solomon said, "The king's favor is as dew upon the grass." In other words, it is "new every morning" (Lam. 3:23). Job, out of his experience, said, "The dew lay all night upon my branch. My glory was fresh in me, and my bow was renewed in my hand" (Job 29:19, 20). Yes, tomorrow is another day, for "his compassions fail not. They are new every morning" (Lam. 3:22, 23). As he restored the vessel in the beginning, so he keeps it a thing of beauty and in repair. Should failure come, there is always a new day with new mercies and a new supply of the dews of his Holy Spirit.

> *Every day is a fresh beginning,*
> *Every morn is the world made new;*
> *You who are weary of sorrow and sinning,*
> *Here is a beautiful hope for you,*
> *A hope for me and a hope for you.*

Remember, tomorrow is another day!

Not only does the Holy Spirit bring restoration as the dew brings life to the plant; but as the dew brings satisfaction and allows the

The Dew of Heaven

thirsty plant to drink, so the Spirit of God alone can bring us satisfaction in life. There is yet another prophetic promise that deals with Jacob and the blessing he is to bring to this world. "The remnant of Jacob shall be in the midst of many people as a dew from the Lord" (Mic. 5:7). Jacob the Supplanter became Israel, the Prince with God and a blessing to his people. This is speaking of a racial, national Jacob who, we believe, some day, when the dews of the Spirit of God have come upon him, will be in the midst of many people as the dew from the Lord, dew that refreshes and satisfies. But until then there is great spiritual blessing for the believer in the realization that the Spirit brings the dews of sustaining satisfaction to him.

When Israel traveled from the Red Sea to the land that had been promised, there were many and varied experiences. Almost at the very beginning they cried out because of lack of food, murmured against God and against his servant Moses; but Moses interceded and sought of God the answer, and the word was given that God would supply manna from heaven. We read that after the night of promise, "when the dew that lay was gone up, behold, upon the face of the wilderness there lay a small round thing. . . . And when the children of Israel saw it, they said one to another, It is manna" (Exod. 16:14, 15). In the morning, as they went out, they saw dew all about them, but no food. But when the sun rose and the dew disappeared, they found underneath the food which God had supplied. Is not this a beautiful revelation of him who said, "I am the bread of life" (John 6:35)? He also said that their fathers had eaten bread in the wilderness and died, but that he was the manna given directly from heaven. Manna can only be given to us, and Christ can only become the bread of life in sustaining power with all the satisfaction that he brings, when the Holy Spirit as dew uncovers for us the reality of this grace.

One may live a long time without bread, but not without water. Jesus, realizing this, said to the woman at the well, "Whosoever drinketh of the water that I shall give him shall never thirst" (John 4:14). It was hard for her to believe, because she was thinking of the natural and he of the spiritual; but to those to whom the Spirit is given, it becomes perfectly plain. We know that the Holy Spirit brings to us that reality, wherein he becomes the water of life. Thus the Holy Spirit once again is revealed in the dew.

The dew fills the place of water in some places. Authorities tell us the amount of dew deposited may be considerable, and in tropical countries is sometimes sufficient to be collected in gutters. Some years ago one of my deacons took me with him to Bermuda, where we had a delightful time. All who have been to this beautiful Atlantic isle remember the glistening white roofs and their gutters. I had supposed the gutters were to drain off rain water, but now realize that they also were for the dew, which is carried off into cisterns. In southern England there are dew ponds on upper levels of the chalk downs, which are used by cattle as a water supply.

Again, we are reminded of the copiousness of the dew of Hermon, and of the Spirit of God in his inexhaustible supply, and that for us there is sustaining satisfaction as the Holy Spirit brings to us the reality of the Lord Jesus Christ as the bread and water of life.

The Holy Spirit as dew brings to us the unannounced and often unconscious satisfaction of spiritual calm. When Hushai counseled Absalom to get enough men to go against his father David, he said: "So shall we come upon him . . . and we will light upon him as the dew falleth on the ground" (2 Sam. 17:12). He is using this figure of speech to show Absalom that the attack must be made quietly, so that it will come entirely as a surprise. The dew forms in the night and no one is conscious of it, for it forms in silence. Just so, we believe, are the workings of the Holy Spirit. Some might refer back to Pentecost and say that was an occasion far from silent; but the birth of the Spirit is always in silence, even though the aftermath may not be.

I believe the workings of the Spirit are done in silence, and beauty. For Jesus said, "He shall not speak of himself" (John 16:13). The dew forms silently; the snow falls in silence; the stars sing together, and yet we do not hear them. The earth flies in its orbit around the sun, but does so in silence, and none of us is conscious thereof. Much harm is often done in trying to force the Spirit to be noisy and vocal. If he chooses to speak in vocal terms and they edify, none should deny; but more beautiful, helpful, and constructive is the silent ministry of the Holy Spirit which makes

46

The Dew of Heaven

us vocal in our enthusiasm for Jesus Christ and to be like him.
"Thou hast the dew of thy youth" (Psa. 110:3). Here the
Psalmist is speaking messianically and prophetically of the King
in his eternal youth, glory, and strength. Marsh quotes Pulsford
as follows:

> *Jesus has the beauty of eternity's morning upon Him
> today and will retain it for ever. As though He were
> but now proceeding from the Father, He wears, un-
> changed, the pledges of His youth. And from the womb
> of the resurrection morning He ascended, in the cloth-
> ing of our glorified humanity. Everlasting morning
> sits upon His brow, and comes forth from Him as the
> regenerative power of all souls. With Him the fresh,
> fragrant morning, the rich, dewy morning, standeth
> still for ever.*

Yes, he has the dew of his youth; but the believer is united into
oneness of life with him, and thus it may be said or should be said
of the believer, "Thou hast the dew of thy youth." The Holy
Spirit brings to us this perennial spiritual youth, with all of its
vigor and enthusiasm. He comes to strengthen us day by day, if
only we will allow him to do so.

That there are lessons taught in the spiritual kingdom from the
realm of Nature is something that can be discovered by a little
careful research. Dew, as we have seen, comes by natural law.
Job, the author of the most scientific book in the Bible, was asked,
"Who hath begotten the drops of dew?" (Job 38:28). God asked
this question, but Job knew the answer, that the Creator is God.
This probably made his companions more confused in the things
which they were unable to answer.

We discover that there are certain requirements in Nature's
law if dew is to be produced. John Aitken, in 1880, added to the
finding of Wells heretofore referred to, and discovered that there
are five things necessary for the formation of dew according to
the laws of Nature. These are: (1) A good radiating surface, by
which he means a surface that can send forth or emit rays as of
heat in all directions. And we have discovered that blades of grass,
leaves on bushes, etc., are good radiating surfaces. (2) A still

47

atmosphere. (3) A clear sky. (4) A thermal insulation. "Thermal" pertains to heat, "determined or measured by heat." To "insulate" means to isolate and, in physics, to separate from other conducting bodies or something that has a heat insulation. (5) Warm, moist ground.

Now comparing the spiritual realm with the natural realm, or spiritual law with natural law, we find that these five things apply. Let us make the comparison as follows: (1) A good radiating surface. Remember that a good radiating surface is one that is able to radiate or emit the rays of heat that it has received during the day. We discovered from physics that a polished, bright surface is not a good radiating surface, but rather one that is dark, tarnished, or roughened. It seems that this is suggestive of the fact that we, each of us, have been exhorted to "look unto the rock whence ye are hewn, and to the hole of the pit whence ye are digged" (Isa. 51:1). The radiating surface is none other than our life or body. "Know ye not that your body is the temple of the Holy Ghost?" (1 Cor. 6:19). The Temple was a large area, in the center of which the Holy Ghost made real the *shekinah* presence of God. Our body, our life, our personality are not only good radiating surfaces upon which the rays of heat from the eternal Sun of Righteousness may be received and afterwards radiated out into the night of darkness and sin all about us, but they are the *only* radiating surface that God has. This ought to bring very somber and careful and thoughtful reflection into our hearts and minds; for without this, the dews of the Holy Spirit cannot be given. (2) A still atmosphere: "In quietness and in confidence shall be your strength: and ye would not" (Isa. 30:15). This is the word that God is speaking to Israel, and in the last words, "Ye would not," he is revealing that instead of quietness and confidence, there was confusion and lack of strength. A still atmosphere is necessary to the formation of dew, and only he who finds quietness and confidence to be his strength has discovered the still atmosphere of the Spirit by which he in his power may come. There must be a holy confidence and quietness in him, and then will the strength of the Spirit be given.

(3) A clear sky. Physicists tell us that a clear sky is absolutely necessary if there is to be dew in the morning. Just so, there must

be no clouds between us and the Savior. John, in describing the baptism of Jesus, said: "I saw the Spirit descending from heaven like a dove, and it abode upon him" (John 1:32). And Stephen said: "Behold, I see the heavens opened, and the Son of man standing on the right hand of God" (Acts 7:56). No, there must be nothing between the soul and the Savior if the dews of the Holy Spirit are to be found in the morning of every experience.

(4) Thermal insulation. We remember that thermal insulation is heat insulation, or isolation; and this law of Nature in the spiritual realm seems to find its complement on the day of Pentecost. We read: "There appeared unto them cloven tongues like as of fire, and it sat upon each of them. And they were all filled with the Holy Ghost" (Acts 2:3, 4). Note that the fire, which signifies heat, sat upon each one of them individually. This is illustrated in the first chapter of the Revelation, where we read of the seven candlesticks. This, as compared with the Old Testament, shows that whereas then there was one candlestick with seven branches, here there are seven individual candlesticks. We believe it signifies that every believer is separate and stands upon his own foundation and is filled individually or is come upon individually by the Holy Spirit, even as they were on the day of Pentecost. This certainly is spiritual thermal insulation.

(5) And, lastly, there must be warm, moist ground. In Matthew 13 Jesus gives the parable of the sower; and we read of the good soil, that "other [seeds] fell into good ground.... He that received seed into the good ground is he that heareth the word, and understandeth it; which also beareth fruit, and bringeth forth, some a hundredfold, some sixty, some thirty" (Matt. 13:8, 23). Thus, when all of these five things are found in the life of the believer, there must be dew of the Holy Spirit. As the natural law is inexorable, so also is the spiritual. Meet the conditions and the results are yours.

In conclusion, let us remember again that the Holy Spirit as dew is a gift from God, and a most peculiar and particular one. Isaac said to Jacob, "God give thee of the dew of heaven." And Jesus said, "Tarry ye ... until ye be endued with power from on high" (Lk. 24:49). If you have believed, you have received God's gift, and the dew from heaven, promised of Isaac to Jacob in the person

of the Holy Spirit, has been given to you from God the Father.
So also the blessings of the dew as the Spirit of God are yours,
restoring the soul, satisfying the life, sufficient for all things. God
reveals himself in nature, and when the revelation is seen through
the eye of the Spirit, it becomes a blessing.

> *The dewdrop in the breeze of morn,*
> *Trembling and sparkling on the thorn,*
> *Falls to the ground, escapes the eye,*
> *Yet mounts on sunbeams to the sky.*

—Montgomery.

Thus, as the dewdrops, caught up by the breeze, fall upon the
leaves and then to the ground, escape the eye, and yet are caught
up by the sunbeam and carried back to the skies, so also will the
dews of the Holy Spirit fall upon your life and, though unnoticed
by man, cause you to ascend on the sunbeams of his grace, that
you may sit in the heavenlies with him.

RIVERS IN THE   4
DESERT PLACES

*"He that believeth on me, as the Scripture hath said,
out of his belly [innermost being] shall flow rivers of
living water."* (John 7:38)

A river is any natural stream of fresh water larger than a brook or
creek which flows in a well-defined channel. Usually it discharges
into another and larger body of water—the ocean, a lake, or
another river. In this definition of a river one sees how it is suggestive and symbolic of life. Every natural stream must have a
source, a well-defined channel or course; it ultimately discharges
itself into a larger body of water and is purposeful in nature, producing certain results as it winds its way to the sea.

Our purpose is to discover the suggestiveness of rivers as mentioned in the Word of God in their teaching of the Holy Spirit and
his ministry. Twenty-three rivers are mentioned in the Bible,
either described directly by their names, such as Pison, Gihon,
Hiddekel, and the Euphrates, the four rivers that flowed out of the
Garden of Eden; or are identified by either the city or country
through which they flow. These are both illustrated in the case of
Naaman the leper, who became greatly concerned that God's
prophet should command him to dip in the muddy waters of
Jordan rather than "Abana and Pharpar, rivers of Damascus."
Another example—the Nile is referred to in the Bible as the River
of the South, and is the southern border of the land which God
gave, under divine charter, to the children of Israel.

Symbols of the Holy Spirit

In our text Jesus definitely connects the rivers of living water with the ministry of the Holy Spirit, for John records, "But this spake he of the Spirit, which they that believe on him should receive: for the Holy Ghost was not yet given; because that Jesus was not yet glorified" (John 7:39). Thus we shall seek to discover the rivers of God's grace as they bring to us the blessings and influences of the Spirit of God.

Every River Must Have a Source

It is interesting to remind oneself of the mighty rivers that are well-known. The largest in volume is the Amazon, although it is exceeded in length by the combined Mississippi and Missouri rivers. This mighty South American river has a drainage area of 2,722,000 square miles, and actually drains four-tenths of that entire continent. Its source is somewhere in a chain of glacier-fed lakes in the Andes of central Peru. From this source it flows 4,000 miles across Peru and Brazil, to enter the Atlantic Ocean at the equator. The entire breadth of its mouth as it enters the Atlantic is 207 statute miles.

In our own country we have the mighty Mississippi, or Indian Great River as it was known and called by the Indians. This, together with its forty tributaries, has an inland waterway of over 15,000 miles in length. The source of the Mississippi is in the lake region of northern Minnesota, and from there it flows onward until it finally empties into the Gulf of Mexico. The Mississippi drains 1,000,240 square miles of land, much less than that which is drained by the Amazon. Many more rivers might be cited; and in each would be found the cause which produces the effect, or the source where the stream begins and without which it could not be.

Turning now to the rivers of God's grace, we discover that these too have a source. The source has been prophesied in the words of Isaiah: "And a man shall be as a hiding place from the wind, and a covert from the tempest; as rivers of water in a dry place, as the shadow of a great rock in a weary land" (Isa. 32:2). The man referred to by Isaiah was not a man of his day or of our day, but was fulfilled by the God-Man who came that he might produce those blessings, described in such prophetic language, spiritually. No other man has ever been the source of such blessing to his fellow-men; indeed, oftentimes so-called great men have been the source and producers of suffering, even as we are witnessing in the world today. It is of this Man the Scripture says: "In the volume of the book it is written of me..." (Psa. 40:7). Probably no explorer has ever discovered the actual place where the Amazon finds its source; he can simply point to the far-off glacier-fed lakes. And yet here is the definite signpost of God, prophesying the actual source from which the rivers of grace will flow.

Those were wonderful words which Jesus spoke on that last great day of the feast, and which are the text of our message. Marsh suggests that we have been wrong in our translation or exegesis which would make the believer the source and gives us Stier's reading, which makes Jesus himself, by his own claim, the source: "If any thirst, let him come unto me; and let him drink, who believeth in me, even as the Scripture has said, Rivers out of him shall flow, of living water." Perhaps this is a new exegesis, although, as with all believers, there is the recognition that waters of eternal life can be given to us only through Jesus Christ.

It has always been a comfort to rest upon the promise that if we believed, from us would flow rivers of living waters. The translation given above does not in any way affect this view, except to greatly enrich in the knowledge that the source to which he would direct all is himself. He is the fount or source from which waters flow. Waters flow from within us, but only by his indwelling. Thus the source of the rivers of God's grace has been completely identified. Men decry doctrine and claim that the things we believe pertaining to Christ are man-made. Such shallow thinkers ought to realize that Christ is the Man who makes the doctrines, even as he has in this particular instance. Without him there is no doctrine.

It will become interesting and instructive to discover the means by which the waters issue and the source is produced. Oftentimes the fountains or springs which are the source of rivers are but water coming through the broken soil or rock. The waters have forced their way through the soil, and this means that there has been an eruption or a smiting. Perhaps in some cataclysmic past, the mighty rivers of our day found their source. Just so is the means by which the source of the rivers of God's grace and of the

Spirit is given. Bear in mind that when Jesus made the foregoing reference, John immediately followed by saying in parenthesis: "but this spake he of the Spirit, which they that believe on him should receive: for the Holy Ghost was not yet given; because that Jesus was not yet glorified."

The Spirit could not be given until Jesus was glorified. He himself said to his disciples, "It is expedient for you that I go away: for if I go not away, the Comforter [Paraclete] will not come unto you; but if I depart, I will send him unto you" (John 16:7). By this he is seeking to teach his disciples that while he is present upon earth in his incarnation, the Holy Spirit must indwell him in all his fullness. Thus, until he has finished this part of his redemptive ministry and returned to the right hand of his Father in glory, the fullness of the Spirit could not be given to them. But he could not be glorified until he was crucified; and having been crucified, he could be glorified. In this we see or discover the source from which these spiritual rivers flow; it was from the crucified or smitten Christ.

This is taught in type through the experience of Moses in the smiting of the rock in Horeb: "I will stand before thee there upon the rock in Horeb; and thou shalt smite the rock" (Exod. 17:6). This is the promise of God, and in obedience to this promise and command Moses smote the rock and the water was given. Paul tells us that the Rock from which they drank and that followed them was Christ. But in reading the account of Israel's wanderings, we find that Moses smote the rock a second time. However, this time God had said: "Take the rod, and gather thou the assembly together . . . and *speak* ye unto the rock before their eyes; and it shall give forth his water" (Num. 20:8). Moses gathered the assembly of the people together, but instead of obeying the strict command of God, he disobeyed in that he smote the rock a second time. God had distinctly said, "Speak to the rock."

This command was given with purpose, for the rock smitten once was a type of Christ smitten once for all upon the cross; and God is teaching that there can be no second smiting, but from the One once crucified the waters will flow and be given when the one in need speaks. This second smiting took place in the land of the Edomites, and it has been my privilege to see the traditional rock from which there flows the only water in that entire vicinity, and which runs down into the Wady Musa, or the Brook of Moses. Whether this is the exact spot or not, no one knows; but at least it is most suggestive.

As mentioned before, Paul definitely connects Christ with this experience of Israel, and refers to him as "that spiritual Rock that followed them: and that Rock was Christ" (1 Cor. 10:4). When his body hung upon the cross, it was pierced by the spear of a Roman soldier, and there gushed forth blood and water. Is it not suggestive that both blood and water appeared? The Word of God tells us that "the life of the flesh is in the blood: . . . for it is the blood that maketh an atonement for the soul" (Lev. 17:11). Thus we are justified, even though our liberal friends abhor the phrase, in singing

> *There is a fountain filled with blood*
> *Drawn from Emmanuel's veins;*
> *And sinners plunged beneath that flood*
> *Lose all their guilty stains.*

But there was also the water, and thus we are also justified in saying that there is another fountain, not of blood but of life-giving waters that flow out from his innermost being. There can be no rivers of God's grace without a source, and the source is clearly identified in Christ, the crucified.

Every River Cuts Its Own Course

If one studies a map of any country, the course of its rivers will be clearly seen. However, perhaps on a relief map one becomes more impressed with the fact that rivers carve their own courses. By the very force of the waters which flow in ever-increasing volume, they carve their way through valleys, around mountains, through forests, and ofttimes even through great mountain ranges. We have our own Grand Canyon and other evidences of the force of such mighty waters as they have literally carved out their way toward the sea. Thousands of years ago Job declared the truth of this statement, "He cutteth out rivers among the rocks" (Job 28:10).

55

Symbols of the Holy Spirit

So the Holy Spirit, like these mighty rivers, is carving out the course of his life in us. Our life may be one of varied experiences that could be described in their analogy to the valleys and the mountain ranges; but ever onward surges the mighty flow of God's grace in his Spirit until it empties into the sea of life.

In nature the Amazon's tidal phenomena offer rather a splendid illustration. We are told that it commences with a roar, constantly increasing, and advances at the rate of from ten to fifteen miles an hour, with the breaking wall of water from five to twelve feet high. Thus it makes its mighty way far into the waters of the Atlantic. In our day engineers have built great reservoirs and mighty dams, such as Boulder Dam and others; and they have had to use the strongest of reenforcements to hold these waters back. Probably they could not be held back if it were not for the fact that a great lake or basin is formed as the waters are dammed up, and thus the ever-rushing current is abated and gives way to the still waters of the great reservoir.

What a comfort and encouragement it ought to be to all of us who are Christians to know that even without our consciousness the Spirit of God as a mighty river is carving out his own course through the varying experiences of our life! Back of the floodgates is the mighty reservoir.

The geologist tells us that in rare instances there may be lost rivers in regions of forest soil, where the water soaks into the ground or, in excessively arid regions, where it evaporates. Under such conditions the river becomes lost. Perhaps this is a warning or reminder to us that the river of God's grace in us may become lost. There is no question that spiritually there is often porous soil or arid regions, and great evaporation. When these conditions are spiritual, then the river may be lost. Perhaps Jesus was referring to something like this, at least by way of intimation, in his parable of the sower:

> Some fell upon stony places, where they had not much earth: and forthwith they sprung up, because they had no deepness of earth: and when the sun was up, they were scorched; and because they had no root, they withered away.... He that received the seed into

> *stony places, the same is he that heareth the word, and
> anon with joy receiveth it; yet hath he not root in
> himself, but dureth for a while: for when tribulation or
> persecution ariseth because of the word, by and by he
> is offended* (Matt. 13:5, 6, 20, 21).

In many places these lost rivers are discovered. In New Hampshire
we have a lost river, and in the New River at Fort Lauderdale,
Florida, there is a place where, in passing on a boat, one can
clearly see the waters literally boiling up in the midst of the stream.
The scientific answer to this is that these waters are forcing their
way out of the mouth of a lost river. The thing that should concern
us is the question, Has the stream of life become a lost river in us
because our faith was but superficial, the soil in which the seed,
the Word of God, was sown porous, the regions of our life arid; or
was there rapid evaporation of the truths received into the
atmosphere?

Again, geologists tell us that rivers as they grow older usually
widen their valleys accordingly, and, of course, with this the
volume of water increases. This should be true of us as we grow
older in the things of the Spirit. Ezekiel's vision of the river that
flowed from under the threshold of the reconstructed Temple of
the millennial day is most suggestive of this. It is described thus:

> *Behold, waters issued out from under the threshold of
> the house eastward: for the forefront of the house
> stood toward the east, and the waters came down from
> under, from the right side of the house, at the south
> side of the altar. Then brought he me out of the way of
> the gate northward, and led me about the way without
> unto the outer gate by the way that looketh eastward;
> and, behold, there ran out waters on the right side.
> And when the man that had the line in his hand went
> forth eastward, he measured a thousand cubits, and
> he brought me through the waters; the waters were to
> the ankles. Again he measured a thousand, and
> brought me through the waters; the waters were to the
> knees. Again he measured a thousand, and brought me
> through; the waters were to the loins. Afterward he*

measured a thousand; and it was a river that I could not pass over: for the waters were risen, waters to swim in, a river that could not be passed over (Ezek. 47:1-5).

Realize that this is a prophetic picture, and yet believe that it is spiritually true, or may be spiritually true in the life of every believer. As the rivers of nature widen with age and increase in the volume of water that flows in them, so the rivers of God's grace as described in the vision of Ezekiel should ever increase until at last they have become a river in which we may swim. When we have come to this place, then we shall know the delights of this divine exercise. Swimming, we are told, exercises all the muscles of the human body. Thus, when we swim in these spiritual waters, our whole spiritual being finds exercise, and with it health and strength.

Every River Is an Instrument of God in Nature

God has a purpose in all things that he created, and this is true of the rivers. As we seek to discover the purpose in Nature of these streams, we shall see how illustrative it is of the rivers of God's Spirit flowing in our life.

In Psalm 1 we read, "Blessed is the man that walketh not in the counsel of the ungodly" (Psa. 1:1), and then follows the description of the fruitfulness of his life: "He shall be like a tree planted by the rivers of water, that bringeth forth his fruit in his season" (Psa. 1:3). This of course is messianic, and the portrait of God's blessed or happy man in his Son Jesus Christ, but it is also true of those who believe and in whom the rivers of God's grace are flowing. The promise is that he will become like a tree planted by the rivers and bring forth his fruit.

As a youngster, I often went canoeing on the Charles River. In the spring the willows and other trees would be very beautiful. Why? Because their roots found food in the bed of the river. The river enriches its bed by depositing soil brought down from the hills; and then, in turn, the roots draw out the nourishment necessary for life. Only as we get our roots in the bed of the river of life-giving waters of his Word can we be fruitful and bring forth our fruit in our season. But this is God's promise to us, and the rivers that flow from Christ will indeed bear fruit in life.

Again, we are told, "There is a river, the streams whereof shall make glad the city of God" (Psa. 46:4). The word that is used for "glad" means literally *glad*, or filled with merriment and delight. This is not mere levity, but there is a sense of real Spirit-borne buoyancy and delight in the life of the one who is Spirit-filled. Such a one has a spontaneous, natural joy about him that enhances the personality and attracts others with magnetism to the Source. Of him it can be said, "A merry heart doeth good like a medicine" (Prov. 17:22).

Jesus said, "Ask, and ye shall receive, that your joy may be full" (John 16:24). This is the joy to which the Psalmist refers; it is a condition that is not dependent upon happenings, but upon the indwelling of the Spirit of God and the outflow of the rivers of his grace. How wonderful it would be if in our attempt to be, as we are instructed by the Apostle, "a peculiar people," we would try to make this our peculiarity—not a somberness and a sadness that oddly make us peculiar but not winsome—but a joy-filled life that will make us peculiar because we are different from other people, and will also make us as magnets, drawing others to the Source in which we find our joy.

Those who live by streams know that they are beneficial in the production of life, for they produce food in the fish that swim therein, and also in the plant life which grows in the bed thereof. Scripture says, "A man shall be... as rivers of water in a dry place" (Isa. 32:2). As we have seen, this is a direct prophecy of Christ. We are dry indeed, and he through the Holy Spirit vivifies; but this is also true of us, for he can cause us to be as rivers that are life-giving. The river in its course produces food, purifies the stagnant places, washes away debris, fertilizes the soil it drains. This we have seen in the mighty Amazon and the Mississippi. Surely we live in a dry place and a thirsty world. God's promise is:

When the poor and needy seek water, and there is none, and their tongue faileth for thirst, I the Lord will hear them, I the God of Israel will not forsake them. I

59

Symbols of the Holy Spirit

will open rivers in high places, and fountains [source of rivers] in the midst of the valleys: I will make the wilderness a pool of water, and the dry lands springs of water (Isa. 41:17, 18).

What a privilege is ours, and what a responsibility too! And we must be careful that there are no barriers in our life which would in any way prevent the rivers of God's grace in his Spirit flowing through us, that we might be life-giving to those with whom we come in contact.

We are the city of God today, for Jesus said, "Ye are . . . a city that is set on an hill" (Matt. 5:14). And for us the promise is true, "There is a river, the streams whereof shall make glad the city of God."

As one reads the history of great cities, it immediately becomes apparent that their greatness is due, in many instances, to the fact that they were built at the mouth of some great river. Take, for instance, New York, which was originally called New Amsterdam. There is much dispute as to the exact history. Probably New York bay and the Hudson River were first discovered by Giovanni de Verrazano, an Italian navigator, in 1524, and seen by Esteban Gomez, a Portuguese, in 1525. However, the most familiar name that history records in connection with New York is Henry Hudson, who in his ship the *Half Moon*, in September 1609 explored the river and really gave New Amsterdam its beginning. New York City has become the greatest city in the world. One reason is because it is so advantageously located at the mouth of the Hudson, and also on New York bay.

Chicago has had remarkable growth. The Chicago River (an Indian name of uncertain origin, but possibly *Ojibwa-she-kagong*, meaning a "wild onion place") was visited by Joliet and Marquette in 1673. It became a portage route of importance. In 1804 the United States established Fort Dearborn at this particular junction or site. In 1831 Chicago was a tiny village, but its growth was immediate and rapid. It is built on the shore of Lake Michigan and a narrow inlet called the Chicago River. This river has been diverted in its course and is now looked upon as an obstruction, but no doubt this stream and harbor greatly affected Chicago's growth and have contributed to its greatness.

Rivers in the Desert Places

So also London has the Thames, Paris has the Seine, and we might continue with many other illustrations. Realizing this, it becomes interesting to note that God's Word says, "The waters made him great, the deep set him up on high with her rivers running round about his plants, and sent out her little rivers unto all the trees of the field" (Ezek. 31:4). As many of the cities of the world have been made great because they have been located at the mouth of or on a mighty river, so individuals can be made great and the rivers of God's grace and Spirit flow out of them. In fact, Jesus said, "A city that is set on an hill cannot be hid" (Matt. 5:14). Was he not teaching that we can be as cities set upon a hill which have become great, or more, that he expects that we shall be.

Learning our lesson from nature, we discover that as great cities of the world have been made great because rivers contributed to their growth, so we too may become great, actual cities of our God as the rivers of life-giving water in the Person of his Holy Spirit find their outlet in our life.

Every River Ultimately Empties into the Sea

In the vision of Ezekiel, we read that the waters "issue out toward the east country, and go down into the desert, and go into the sea: which being brought forth into the sea, the waters shall be healed" (Ezek. 47:8). There is no doubt that the reference here is to the Dead Sea, which is east from Jerusalem, and that in that millennial day the waters from the Temple will flow down the steep descent from the mountains of Jerusalem to the Dead Sea and bring healing to its now lifeless waters. In Ecclesiastes we read, "All the rivers run into the sea" (1:7). This is scientifically true, for while a river may primarily empty itself into a larger body or pond or lake, yet this water finds its outlet into some other river or water course and ultimately makes its way into the sea.

It will be interesting and instructive for us to discover the use of the term "sea" in its scriptural interpretation. Bible interpreters generally agree that when reference in the Bible is made to "the land," it is to the land of Palestine, not necessarily according to its present-day boundaries but as God gave it under divine charter to Abraham, from the Euphrates on the north to the

Nile on the south. In the Revelation we read, "And I beheld another beast coming up out of the earth; and he had two horns like a lamb, and he spake as a dragon" (13:11). This is a false lamb, and therefore a reference to the Antichrist. Notice that he comes up out of the earth. Most of those who teach Bible prophecy are agreed that Antichrist must arise in the land of Palestine; and so the reference "out of the earth" is exact.

Coming to the use of the word "sea," we again find a reference in the Revelation: "And I stood upon the sand of the sea, and saw a beast rise up out of the sea, having seven heads and ten horns" (13:1). Both of these references are in the same chapter, and this latter one appears first. This beast is the first to arise, and is to be a political leader. He arises out of the sea, which symbolizes humanity. When reference is made to the sea in Old Testament prophecy, it is to the sea of humanity, as it is often made today. The terminus of the rivers which flow out of Christ and eventually make their way into the sea are flowing not into the seven seas but into the sea of humanity, which certainly is dead and lifeless in its sinful condition.

As the waters in Ezekiel's vision issue out of the Temple, flow down toward the east, and give life to the waters of the Dead Sea, so the waters of eternal life which flow out from Christ in the presence of his outflowing Spirit flow that they may give life to the dead sea of humanity. But this is not only from Christ, but also from those who are his. He said, "Out of him," referring to himself. But he lives in us, and so as the waters flow out of him, they must in turn flow out of us, and as they flow out of us, it must be life-giving and with healing. As the waters of the mighty Amazon increase in volume and rush into the ocean with a great tidal wave, so there will be in us an ever-increasing volume of the waters of the Holy Spirit. Ours is but to be the bed of the stream; the Spirit of God will carve out his own course in ever-increasing volume, and with it the blessings that heal, fructify, and make great.

Once again we have discovered God in Nature. It is hard to understand how the unbeliever can resist such evidence and continue in his spiritual blindness. But once again the Word of God is confirmed: "The invisible things of him from the creation of the world are clearly seen" (Rom. 1:20), so that all mankind is without excuse. The Negro spiritual sings about "Old Man River," and to some it is a message of fear, anxiety and death; but to the believer the river becomes a messenger of God's blessing. Surely the rivers of God's grace speak forth his message to us.

Let us remember that the vision is for us as well as for the future, and the waters, being first up to the ankles, will increase in depth to the knees, then the loins, and finally become a river to swim in. The promise of God has been given, the Lord Jesus Christ has identified himself as the Source from which the waters flow. He has been glorified, and the Spirit has been given; and we know that "if any man thirst, let him come unto me, and let him drink who believeth in me, even as the Scripture [concerning him] has said, Rivers out of him shall flow of living water." He is indeed the fountain source from which the waters flow; through the indwelling of his own divine Spirit he has brought the issues of these waters to us, and in turn they may flow out from Christ within. "Christ liveth in me."

> *Like a river glorious is God's perfect peace,*
> *Over all victorious in its bright increase.*
> *Perfect—yet it floweth, fuller every day;*
> *Perfect—yet it groweth, deeper all the way.*
>
> *Stayed upon Jehovah, hearts are fully blest,*
> *Finding, as He promised, perfect peace and rest.*
>
> *Hidden in the hollow of His blessed hand,*
> *Never foe can follow, never traitor stand.*
> *Not a surge of worry, not a shade of care,*
> *Not a blast of hurry, touch the spirit there.*
>
> *Every joy or trial falleth from above,*
> *Traced upon our dial by the Sun of Love.*
> *We may trust Him solely, all for us to do;*
> *They who trust Him wholly, find Him wholly true.*
>
> *Stayed upon Jehovah, hearts are fully blessed,*
> *Finding as He promised, perfect peace and rest.*

RAINDROPS OF GLORY 5

"If ye walk in my statues, and keep my command-
ments, and do them; then I will give you rain in due
season, and the land shall yield her increase, and the
trees of the field shall yield their fruit." (Leviticus
26:3, 4)

As we pursue our study of rain with its scriptural parallel in the
giving of the Holy Spirit, it would be well for us to familiarize
ourselves, at least to a small degree, with the science of meteorology. This comes from the Greek word, *metewpa*, meaning the
science of things in the higher air. In its widest sense, the term
includes the study of the weather, climate, optical phenomena in
the atmosphere, and atmospheric electricity.

Real study of meteorology began around the beginning of the
seventeenth century when, in 1607, Galileo invented the thermometer. This was followed by the invention of the barometer in
1643 by Torricelli. Among the first weather charts ever issued
were those by a Bostonian named Estes. He published a service
of daily synchronous observations, and later made valuable
detailed studies. By 1850 many countries had established weather
observation stations, and international cooperation was established by a conference held in Brussels in 1853. This international
service was later put upon a sound basis by a congress held in
Vienna in 1873.

Today, with governmental departments, it has become almost an exact science. Living in one world, as we do, with radio, telegraphy, and many other modern devices by which information is transmitted, knowledge of the weather conditions in all parts of the world is at hand through this international service.

But there is also a spiritual meteorology, as we discover in this study and many of the others with which we are dealing. It is interesting to note that many of the figures of speech or parallels used in Scripture fit within this particular realm of science. In the spiritual meteorology, as we have called it, it is our purpose to discover natural law revealing the truths of the Spirit. While we know that such insight does not come until one has the mind and understanding of the Holy Spirit, yet the things of God's creation are irrefutable testimony against all who would plead ignorant of any revelation of himself.

In many respects rainfall is the most important of all meteorological elements. At the same time, it is one of the most difficult to determine exactly. In the revelation of God, rain is very definitely illustrative of the workings of the Holy Spirit in and upon the lives of believers, and may be determined by the exact science of the Word. Leviticus 26:3, 4—"If ye walk in my statutes . . . then I will give you rain in due season." Thus we shall pursue our study of raindrops of glory.

The Source from Which Rain Comes

To the believer, rain is the gift of a beneficent Creator. Eliphaz in his first discourse, as he, with the other two of Job's so-called comforters, speaks to Job, utters these words: "I would seek unto God, and unto God would I commit my cause: which doeth great things and unsearchable; marvelous things without number: Who giveth rain upon the earth, and sendeth waters upon the fields" (Job 5:8-10).

The meteorologist will rightly say that rain comes as the inevitable result of certain fixed natural laws. With this we are willing to agree, of course with this exception—that God can employ a higher law, as he has employed it many times. There have been many evidences of this application of a higher law by God on behalf of humanity. Agreeing with these scientists, we would ask,

Symbols of the Holy Spirit

Who, if not God, made these natural laws? This is the premise of Eliphaz, and it is the premise of every believer in every day.

So also we discover that God is the Giver of the rains of his divine Spirit. Jesus said, "I will pray the Father, and he shall give you another Comforter" (John 14:16). He is the Giver of every good and perfect gift, and the most perfect gift of all is the gift of his Holy Spirit, the divine Paraclete.

Davis, in his *Bible Dictionary*, tells us:

> *From earliest times, besides the solar year, there has been a civil or agricultural year, which began in the autumn. It was convenient for a people devoted to horticulture and agriculture to begin the year with the season of plowing and sowing.*

There are three principal rains or seasons of rain in Palestine, and each of these is significant. In Hosea 6:3 we read: "He shall come unto us as the rain, as the latter and former rain upon the earth." A definite reference to the three rains is found in Joel 2:23, translated by Moffatt as follows: "For the early rain [*moreh*] he has given you amply, the winter rain [*geshem*] he has poured upon you, and sent the latter rain [*malkosh*] as of old." This clearly defines the three principal rains found in the land of Palestine. Now we will see how suggestive these seasonable rains are of the threefold work of God's Spirit.

First, there was the early rain (*moreh*). "The early rain he has given you amply." This was rain in the autumn, beginning in October. It made possible the plowing of the soil and planting of the seed. Just enough rain fell to moisten the ground, which had been baked hard by the unclouded sunshine of the Palestinian summer. Thus does the Holy Spirit fallow the ground of an unregenerate heart and life. He comes gently like the early rains of a Palestinian autumn, in order that the soil might be moistened, the plow of conviction break it up, and the seed of the gospel be planted.

Then come the heavy rains. These are the winter downpours, continuing from December to March. These soak the earth and fill the empty cisterns, making possible the full growth of the seed which has been planted. This rain is called *geshem*. And in the scriptural parallel this illustrates the mighty supply of the Spirit's power that becomes real in experience when after the sowing of the seed and conversion, the life is completely surrendered to Jesus Christ and he becomes Lord of all. When we have reached this place by the downpour of the Spirit of God, the seed which has been sown grows into the full, well-nourished sturdy plant.

Then there is the latter rain, *malkosh*. These latter, or spring, rains cause the ear to fill out and withstand the terrific drought that comes just before the harvest. This last is light rain from mid-March until the dry season sets in in late April or May. Is not this a revelation of the constant, unannounced, yet ever-continuing work of the Spirit of God as he brings forth the full ear or the complete results of his indwelling and sanctification? This is ever-increasing as we near the dry season or the ending of things mortal, that the harvest might be abundant.

Paul must have been thinking of something like this when he said, "We all, with open face beholding as in a glass the glory of the Lord, are changed into the same image from glory to glory, even as by the Spirit of the Lord" (2 Cor. 3:18). Christian experience may be more or less stationary or static, but it is not supposed to be, and does not need to be, for God has given promise: "For the early rain he has given you amply, the winter rain he has poured upon you, and sent the latter rain as of old." In other words, God has done his part to make possible the sowing of the seed, the development or growth of the plant, and the rich and abundant harvest. If these things are not realities in our life, then the above verse will disclose the answer as to why they are not.

The Promise and the Condition

Showers of God's blessing were promised to Israel. "If ye walk in my statutes, and keep my commandments, and do them; then I will give you rain in due season, and the land shall yield her increase and the trees of the field shall yield their fruit" (Lev. 26:3, 4). This can be proven by the pages of history, for when Israel walked in his statutes and kept his commandments, he gave abundant blessing and they were fruitful and used of God. When they departed from his commandments, they were an enigma and far from the blessings that God had promised.

This is given not only unto Israel, but unto all who believe, and applies to your life and mine. God's instruction was that they should walk in his statutes and keep his commandments; and we need to discover that this law governs the influence of the Holy Spirit upon our life. Just as natural laws govern and control the giving of rain, so also are the spiritual laws. If we fulfill them, the rains of the Holy Spirit must come. There is no other alternative.

The reference is first of all to "statutes" that must be kept. These were laws enacted by force of circumstances. There are statutes which the Holy Spirit dictates to us. Each one receives this dictation individually, by the still, small voice of the Spirit of God or through his Word; and sometimes collectively. The Psalmist said, "If I regard iniquity in my heart, the Lord will not hear me" (Psa. 66:18). People often wonder why the Spirit of God does not make possible the answer to their prayer. Perhaps it is because they have not walked in this statute, which is but one.

Seeking the blessing of the Spirit of God is similar to seeking redress in a court of equity. It is a law of equity that he who seeks relief therefrom must come to the court with clean hands. It is a statute or law of God that he who seeks the blessing of the Spirit must fulfill or obey the statutes which he has given.

There are the "commandments" which must be kept also. These are the things which are necessary to the very existence of humanity and to all of God's children. Jesus, when questioned by the lawyer or scribe who asked, "Master, which is the greatest commandment in the law?" (Matt. 22:36), summed these up. He answered, "Thou shalt love the Lord thy God with all thy heart, and with all thy soul, and with all thy mind. This is the first and great commandment. And the second is like unto it, Thou shalt love thy neighbor as thyself" (Matt. 22:37-39). In other words, Jesus is saying that love, complete and unreserved toward God; love by the indwelling of the Spirit of God, complete and unreserved toward him; love by the Spirit of God toward others, even

the unlovely and the unloving, is absolutely essential if we are to
have the full blessing of the indwelling Spirit.

> *True love shall trust, but selfish love must die,*
> *For trust is peace, and self is full of pain;*
> *Arise and heal thy brother's grief; his tears*
> *Shall wash thy love, and it will live again.*
> —J. B. O'Reilly.

After all, this was the great purpose of God in Israel, and involved in this is the keeping of the commandments and the walking
in his statutes. In the spiritual realm the application is to you and
to me. Meet God's demands, and it will be his delight to give the
blessing.

Raindrops of Glory

I like to think of the blessings of the Holy Spirit as revealed in
the rain as raindrops of glory; for, after all, it is the purpose of the
Spirit to give to us and reveal in us the glory of the risen Christ.

Rain is given in a plenteous supply. "Thou, O God, didst send a
plentiful rain, whereby thou didst confirm thine inheritance, when
it was weary" (Psa. 68:9). "Plentiful" means copious, or full
supply. And as God gave full supply of rain to the land of Palestine, so he does to every believer; for we have received of "his
fullness." The supply is plentiful, as much as the vessel can hold;
for he says, "Be filled with the Spirit." When we empty the vessel
of debris, we are able to fill it with rain water.

A former associate, Rev. A. B. Webber, has a small place on the
coast of Maine. It is not possible to have town water, and therefore
a pump is used. Visiting him one time, I washed my hands at the
sink and found the water to be very soft, creating an easy lather
from soap. I discovered that for washing they use rain water,
which is conveyed through gutters to a cistern in which it is stored.
Leaves and other things that fall into the cistern during the winter
must be cleaned out before it may be used again.

Thus, in our life it will be necessary that we clear away all the
debris, if we would have the complete filling of the Holy Spirit.

69

Symbols of the Holy Spirit

The Holy Spirit, being a divine personality, has been given to us in all his fullness; for he could not be given in any other way. But even though we may be possessed of his fullness, he may not be possessing us in our fullness. We can be filled, for we have received a copious and full supply of spiritual rain in his coming.

The Word of God suggests that rain is refreshing and cleansing as it falls. "He watereth the hills from his chambers: the earth is satisfied with the fruit of thy works" (Psa. 104:13). We have already seen the function of rains and their relationship to Palestinian agriculture; and all of us have known the refreshing of a shower in the humidity of summer. By the rain God drives away humidity, waters the earth, cleans the atmosphere, and washes his creation. Dr. William Stidger's very beautiful poem, "I Saw God Wash the World," is most suggestive of this relationship:

> I saw God wash the world last night
>   With His sweet showers on high;
> And then when morning came
>   I saw Him hang it out to dry.
>
> He washed each slender blade of grass,
>   And every trembling tree;
> He flung His showers against the hills
>   And swept the rolling sea.
>
> The white rose is a deeper white;
>   The red, a richer red
> Since God washed every fragrant face
>   And put them all to bed.
>
> There's not a bird, there's not a bee
>   That wings along the way,
> But is a cleaner bird and bee
>   Than it was yesterday.
>
> I saw God wash the world last night;
>   Ah, would He had washed me
> As clean of all my dust and dirt
>   As that old white birch tree!

Paul says, "But ye are washed, . . . in the name of the Lord Jesus, and by the Spirit of our God" (1 Cor. 6:11). Thus, as God washes the world by the rains that fall, so he washes us by his Spirit.

We have already seen that rain is seasonal; but it will be instructive to discover that it is also timely in its coming. There are the regularities of the seasons, and God's promise to Noah is still true: "While the earth remaineth, seedtime and harvest, and cold and heat, and summer and winter, and day and night shall not cease" (Gen. 8:22). This we may rely upon because of the constancy and faithfulness of the One who made the promise.

In the promise of these various seasons and conditions, there is involved the promise of the weather which may be expected. Thus we have the timely rains, coming in the regularity of their seasons: the former, the heavy, and the latter rains. This is true, as we have already seen, in the experience of the believer, or perhaps we should say, may be true in the experience of the believer. Once again, remember—as we meet the conditions laid down by spiritual law, God has no other alternative.

There is also an intermittent timeliness to the giving of rain. "The Lord shall open unto thee his good treasure, the heaven to give the rain unto thy land in his season" (Deut. 28:12). This is the promise of God to Israel. In the time of Ahab, rain was given after the period of drought; and Elijah's conversation and instructions to Ahab are revealing, to say the least. "And Elijah the Tishbite . . . said unto Ahab . . . There shall not be dew nor rain these years, but according to my word" (1 Kings 17:1). After the contest with the prophets of Baal, Elijah said to Ahab, "Get thee up, eat and drink; for there is a sound of abundance of rain" (1 Kings 18:41). Elijah went to the top of Carmel, put his face in his knees, and said to his servant:

> *Go up now, look toward the sea. And he went up, and looked, and said, There is nothing. And he said, Go again seven times. And it came to pass at the seventh time, that he said, Behold, there ariseth a little cloud out of the sea, like a man's hand. And he said, Go up, say unto Ahab, Prepare thy chariot, and get thee down, that the rain stop thee not. And it came to pass in the mean while, that the heaven was black with*

clouds and wind, and there was a great rain. And
Ahab rode, and went to Jezreel (1 Kings 18:43-45).

The servant saw a cloud over the sea the size of a man's hand; this was the promise of the coming rain. Is it too much to say that raindrops of glory come from the fount of another hand, the pierced hand of the Man of Galilee? These are the hands of the Creator, the Redeemer, and the Governor of this universe in which we live. He will give not only the seasonal rain, but also the intermittent, the timely, rain in the moment even though meteorologists might say that weather conditions, atmospheric conditions, etc., all signified fair weather. God can and does apply higher laws, both in the realm of nature and of the spirit.

Rain may be given sparsely or plentifully, according to the conditions that prevail. Thus the blessings of the Holy Spirit may be so determined or governed.

For the land, whither thou goest in to possess it, is not
as the land of Egypt, from whence ye came out, where
thou sowedst thy seed, and wateredst it with thy foot,
as a garden of herbs: But the land, whither ye go to
possess it, is a land of hills and valleys, and drinketh
water of the rain of heaven (Deut. 11:10, 11).

The land the Israelites had left behind was a land of complete barrenness, economically and spiritually. The clay used to make bricks was very hard because of the lack of moisture. For months there is no rain in the land. God's promise was that rain would be plentiful in the land of Canaan, toward which they journeyed.

Their hope was to possess the land. However, possession was delayed for many years by their failure at Kadesh-Barnea. Within sight of the land and on the threshold of its blessings and fertility, they were turned back. This is so much like the experience of the believer. We have been delivered from the land of midnight and bondage and spiritual darkness, and we are in the wilderness journey, having passed through the Red Sea experience, through the various experiences typified by the children of Israel. But when we reach Kadesh-Barnea and the edge of Jordan and the privilege of going in, we listen to the still, small voice, not of our

72

Caleb and Joshua, but of the spies who would hinder the possession of the land; the whisperings of Satan, instead of the tri-
umphant note of the eternal God.

We turn back to years of wilderness wanderings, when we might
go over immediately and possess the land and find that in possessing it every obstacle would be overcome, every enemy subdued,
every walled city taken, and that we could plow the fertile soil of
our Christian experience, sowing the seed and reaping an abundant harvest. When Israel finally entered the land and sought to
prove God, the word is given: "There failed not aught of any good
thing which the Lord had spoken unto the house of Israel; all came
to pass" (Josh. 21:45). This may be true with you and me. "But
the land, whither ye go to possess it, is a land of hills and valleys,
and drinketh water of the rain of heaven" (Deut. 11:11).

Raindrops May Become Floods of Judgment

So far we have been considering that which is pleasing in the
blessings of the Holy Spirit, but we cannot set our study aside until
we face the teachings of the Word that as rain can be the instrument or minister of judgment in the hand of God, so the Spirit may
also. In Noah's day the rain was that instrument of judgment:
"God saw that the wickedness of man was great.... And it re-
pented the Lord that he had made man.... And the Lord said, I
will destroy.... I will cause it to rain upon the earth forty days
and forty nights" (Gen. 6:5-7; 7:4). The Flood is a thing of the
past, and the promise is that the world will never know another
flood of such severity.

But with the rains or floods of God's judgment in the Holy
Spirit, this may not be. Jesus, in the promise of the Spirit's
coming, said, "When he is come, he will reprove the world of sin,
and of righteousness, and of judgment" (John 16:8). Not only is
he the Supplier of divine life in regeneration, but he may be the
messenger of severity and judgment to both the believer and the
unbeliever. Again, the world must hear the words of the prophet:
"Return, thou backsliding Israel, saith the Lord; and I will not
cause mine anger to fall upon you" (Jer. 3:12).

Symbols of the Holy Spirit

Perhaps the rains of God will come upon you in your insecure foundation.

> *Therefore whosoever heareth these sayings of mine, and doeth them, I will liken him unto a wise man, which built his house upon a rock: And the rain descended, and the floods came, and the winds blew, and beat upon that house; and it fell not: for it was founded upon a rock. And every one that heareth these sayings of mine, and doeth them not, shall be likened unto a foolish man, which built his house upon the sand: And the rain descended, and the floods came, and the winds blew, and beat upon that house; and it fell: and great was the fall of it* (Matt. 7:24-27).

Here Jesus parallels the rains which descended in floods and destroyed the house built on the sands to the judgment which must come to all who are not building upon a sure foundation. Paul said, "Other foundation can no man lay than that is laid, which is Jesus Christ" (1 Cor. 3:11). He who builds on Christ is wise and need have no fear; for the rains of judgment can never blast away the house built thereon.

In conclusion, let us remember that as the science of meteorology proves certain conditions are essential to the giving of rain, so there is the divine science by which we discover the condition necessary to the giving and blessing of his Spirit.

Galileo gave us the thermometer, an instrument for measuring temperature. Rain falls only when the tempeature is above freezing, and by using the spiritual thermometer of the Word we soon determine that there must be warmth, the warmth of his love and of his Spirit, in our souls if we are to have raindrops of glory.

It was Torricelli who gave us the barometer. This is an instrument for indicating atmospheric pressure. We need a spiritual barometer to determine that at all times there is the proper atmospheric pressure in the Spirit, so that there may be raindrops of glory. If we meet God's law, the raindrops will be ours.

> *If ye walk in my statutes, and keep my commandments, and do them; then I will give you rain in due*

Raindrops of Glory

season, and the land shall yield her increase, and the trees of the field shall yield their fruit.... I will give peace in the land, and ye shall lie down, and none shall make you afraid (Lev. 26:3, 4, 6).

God has given abundance of rain in the fullness of the Spirit.

Showers there are for the thirsty soul,
A sweet and refreshing dew;
The Spirit who makes the wounded whole
And the evil heart makes new.

He will teach the trembling one to cling
To an arm of love and might;
And the earth-stained soul 'neath his holy wing
Shall again be pure and white.

The weary heart with its wild unrest
He can hush to a trustful calm;
To the spirit crushed and sorely pressed
He comes with his healing balm.

He comes to the soul in its sin-wrought tomb
And rent are the chains of death!
Then his own sweet graces awake and bloom
Beneath his living breath.

Yes! The Spirit shall teach the heart to sing,
And shall tune its long-silent lyre,
And he who shall meeten it praise to bring
In the sinless, white-robed choir.

Come then, O Spirit, as once of yore,
Come in thy quickening might!
Come, on thy waiting Church to pour
Thy life, thy grace, thy light!

HOW DEEP THE SNOW!   6

"Hast thou entered into the treasures of the snow? or hast thou seen the treasures of the hail?" (Job 38:22)

After Job's three friends had sought vainly to commiserate him in his forsaken condition, the Lord intervened and answered Job out of the whirlwind. These four chapters of the Lord's message to him are filled with statements which the wise men of every age must face and answer. Now, the Scriptures do not profess to be a scientific textbook, yet whenever they speak on scientific subjects, they speak with exactness.

The questions asked by the Lord of Job still challenge the minds of thinking men. One question in particular suggests our text: "Hast thou entered into the treasures of the snow?" To those who live in a latitude where snow is common, it will be interesting to discover spiritual lessons as well as economic values. To those who live in climates where snow is never seen except perhaps on a picture postcard, the study will prove itself not only instructive but entrancing, and perhaps create a longing for a trip to the north.

Once again we let God speak to us out of the universe of his creation. Boreham, in one of his books, *I Forgot To Say*, has this to say about the things of Nature:

> *Human verdicts are hasty and harsh and pitiless; but God is light; and, in the whole of the universe, there is nothing so gentle as light. The Bible is amazingly rich*

76

How Deep the Snow!

in its symbolism of tenderness. It likens the gentleness of God to the gentleness of the snowflake as it flutters silently to the ground; to the soft down on the breast of a mother-bird; to the dew as it sparkles on the grass. And each of these emblems is wonderfully eloquent and appealing. The snow is so gentle that a million tons, falling in a night, make less noise than the rustling of a leaf or the scamper of a mouse. Yet the weight of the snow eventually crushes trees and buildings and birds and beasts, whilst it sets in motion the avalanche that leaves in its wake a trail of havoc and disaster. The mother-bird's soft breast has been known to suffocate her tiny offspring; whilst even the tiny weight of the dewdrop is a strain on the strength of the slenderest blade.

How blind we humans are, that so oftentimes we close our eyes to the things God is seeking to teach through these instruments of his creation! The snow is one of God's treasure houses, and out of it we shall seek to bring forth its riches.

Out of the bosom of the air,
Out of the cloud-folds of her garments shaken,
Over the woodlands brown and bare,
Over the harvest-fields forsaken,
  Silent, and soft and slow
  Descends the snow.
                              —Longfellow, "Snowflakes."

The Divine Source

The meteorologist tells us snow is but water vapor in the air, crystallized into geometrical forms; that it forms usually within, below, or between cloud strata and at various heights within the atmosphere, according to the latitude and the temperature prevailing within the clouds. Agreed; but who, if not God, is the Creator of such conditions? Elihu, one of his comforters, said to Job: "He saith to the snow, Be thou on the earth" (Job 37:6). Behind all the laws of nature the Christian sees the hand and mind of God. "The Lord answered Job out of the whirlwind and said:

> *Where wast thou when I laid the foundations of the earth? declare, if thou hast understanding. Who hath laid the measures thereof, if thou knowest? or who hath stretched the line upon it? Whereupon are the foundations thereof fastened? or who laid the corner stone thereof; when the morning stars sang together, and all the sons of God shouted for joy?* (Job 38:1, 4-7).

Again we would ask the question, Who, if not the Son of God, still governs the universe of Nature? Paul, in his Colossian letter, says that all things were created for him and by him, and "by him all things consist" (1:17). Perhaps a better translation is, "In him all things have their harmonious whole." To the Christian the world is Christocentric, not only in the realm of the Spirit but also in the realm of Nature and the universe at large. Thus Elihu spoke words of truth when he said, God "saith to the snow, Be thou on the earth."

Drawing our spiritual parallel between the snow and the Holy Spirit, we discover the source of this gift of God. As noted in other chapters, God himself is the source. Jesus said to his disciples, "I will pray the Father, and he shall give you another Comforter ... even the Spirit of truth" (John 14:16, 17). It was to these disciples that he had said it would be expedient for him to go away, because in his going it would be possible for the Spirit to be given. The only source of spiritual wisdom and understanding and power is from the Holy Spirit, and he comes only from the presence of God.

As the snow, according to the meteorologist, comes from the high altitudes and as water vapor in the air crystallizes in geometrical form, so the Holy Spirit is the spiritually crystallized personality of the Lord Jesus Christ, coming to us from the high altitudes of heaven and the presence of God himself. This is divine science.

The Region of the Snow

Snow is perennial on certain mountaintops, and the meteorologists speak of the snow line. This is the line above which the

How Deep the Snow!

snow remains unmelted in the form of a permanent snow field. In Lapland it is 4,000 feet above sea level; in the Alps it is 9,000 feet; in the Himalayas, 13,000 feet on the south side and 16,500 feet on the north side; and at the equator it is 18,000 feet. Here it is that the eye sees a perennial field of snow covering the tops of the mountains. Below this line the snow disappears.

There is what we might designate the spiritual region of the perennial snows of the Holy Spirit, spiritual mountaintops where his presence is always known in experience. Paul tells us that we have been "blessed with all spiritual blessings in heavenly places in Christ" (Eph. 1:3). This is our positional relationship in Christ, but also our experiential relationship. He, in experience, may be perennial when we dwell upon the mountaintops.

> God hath his mountains bleak and bare,
>   Where he doth bid us rest awhile;
> Crags where we breathe a purer air,
>   Lone peaks that catch the day's first smile.

As with climatic conditions the permanency varies or depends, so it may be that we shall have to go higher in our relationship with him. "Seek those things which are above" (Col. 3:1), if you would know the perennial blessing of the Holy Spirit.

The Poor Man's Riches

Once again we hear the question of the Lord to Job, "Hast thou entered into the treasures of the snow?" At first glance, this seems to be a statement with little scientific significance or spiritual value, and yet further study would show how erroneous such a view is.

Nature, by her laws and with the use of snow, rehabilitates the soil. Dr. Harry Rimmer, in his book *The Harmony of Science and Scripture*, wrote years ago:

> *What can possibly be the treasure that is connected with snow and with hail? We don't believe Job knew, and certainly no modern writer or reader knew until Dr. Frank T. Shutt, Dominion chemist of the Canadian Department of Agriculture, published the result*

79

of his seventeen years of research in the financial worth of snow and hail.

In a recent issue "Science," a release by "Science Service," recounts the result of Dr. Shutt's experiments. He finds that there is a definite financial value to snow and hail, as they wash out of the atmosphere nitrogenous substances that fertilize the soil. The action of snow and hail, centrifuging through the air, deposits upon the land four kinds of chemical fertilizer: free ammonia, nitrates, nitrites, and albuminoid ammonia. These substances, to the value of $14.08 per acre, are deposited in a winter's fall of snow and hail. These are the forms in which the nitrogen of the air can be assimilated by plants as food. This is the equivalent of forty-four pounds of expensive imported Chilean saltpeter per acre.

If a farmer had ten acres of land under cultivation, the treasure of the snow and the hail for him would be $140.80 per year. If you ascertain the number of acres under cultivation in your state and multiply them by $14.08 per acre, you will learn what the treasure of the snow and the hail really amounts to in your locality.

If you multiply the number of arable acres in North America by this factor, you will get a stupendous sum of real money!

In a radio message many years ago I mentioned this rehabilitation of the soil by snow, and was challenged by a farmer who had been listening in. He said if it were true, he had never observed it. Scientific data was sent to him proving the exactness of the statement, and that he had been the recipient of natural fertilizer to the saving of hundreds of dollars. The farmer could well be asked, "Hast thou entered into the treasures of the snow?"

Snow, symbolizing to us the ministry of the Holy Spirit in its power to rehabilitate the soil, reveals to us how the Spirit of God rehabilitates the soul of man. "The inward man is renewed day by day" (2 Cor. 4:16). And Titus tells us, "Not by works of righteousness which we have done, but according to his mercy he saved us, by the washing of regeneration, and renewing of the Holy Ghost" (Tit. 3:5). There is this daily or momentary renewing of the Spirit of God, by which each of us is rehabilitated in our life. As Nature rehabilitates the soil with its gift of snow, so God rehabilitates the soul by the renewing of the Holy Spirit. When it seems as though the very best in us has been completely used up, God gives us this renewing or spiritual rejuvenation or rehabilitation, so that we are able to go on with added strength.

One thinks of the words of Jeremiah in Lamentations, "It is of the Lord's mercies that we are not consumed, because his compassions fail not. They are new every morning: great is thy faithfulness" (Lam. 3:22, 23). The Christian does not need to wait until the season of the year when snow is given, as the farmer must for the rehabilitation of his soil; but every moment, by the surrender of life, he may find the renewing of the Holy Spirit and the rehabilitation of his soul.

Drawing the analogy between the snow and the Holy Spirit to a little greater length, we discover that both of them defy computation. The formation and deposit of the snow, occurring over so large a portion of the earth's surface and in such enormous quantities, is immeasurable. We have been told that twelve inches of snow when melted equals one inch of rain. The snow falls silently, and in a short time it makes its way into every crevice and spot where it has fallen and accumulates to such a depth that it cannot be computed. Computation might be possible in a limited sense and in a limited area; but when we think of the entire amount of snow on the earth's surface, we see how utterly impossible any exact reckoning would be. There is no place on a mountain crag or in a valley where the snow does not make its way and completely cover the area in which it has fallen. Emerson, in his beautiful poem, "Snow Bound," calls the snow the "north-wind's masonry," and shows how this is true:

> *Come see the north-wind's masonry.*
> *Out of an unseen quarry evermore*
> *Furnished with tide, the fierce artificer*
> *Curves his white bastions with projected roof*
> *Round every windward stake, or tree, or door.*

Symbols of the Holy Spirit

Speeding, the myriad-handed, his wild work
So fanciful, so savage, naught cares he
For number or proportion.

In speaking of his own experience, Jesus said, "He that hath received his testimony hath set to his seal that God is true. For he whom God hath sent speaketh the words of God: for God giveth not the Spirit by measure" (John 3:33, 34). If this is true of the gift of the Holy Spirit to the Son of man, it is also true of God's gift of the Spirit to us. No man can compute the measure of the Holy Spirit, for "of his fulness have all we received" (John 1:16). No one ever yet has been able to measure or determine the fullness of the Spirit of God, who is the power and energy and enablement of the Godhead, and of every believer. As the snow completely blankets the earth, finding its way into every nook and cranny and crevice and space, so the Holy Spirit will completely fill us if we but meet the conditions which make his filling possible. He gives and gives and gives again. There is no measure to his giving.

Sometime when you are shoveling your way out from your garage to the street, and the snow has drifted all about you to a great depth, and with your aching back you are just about ready to give up in despair, try to remember this analogy—that even as you cannot compute the depth of the snow in your own back-yard and are about ready to curse it in its coming, there is a greater lesson it is seeking to teach: that in you the Spirit of God will be given far beyond the possibility of any human computation.

The Artistry of God

Snow contains in itself the divine artistry. Snowflakes are treasures in God's museum. At the Agassiz Museum at Harvard College can be seen beautiful glass flowers, made with such skill that they can hardly be distinguished from the real. Every visitor to Boston ought to cross the Charles River into Cambridge and go through this museum. In fact, one who did not do so would be justified in feeling that he had missed one of the important places of interest. But how often do we, in the midst of a snowstorm, see not the artificial but the real, directly as it comes from the hand of God!

How Deep the Snow!

For many years naturalists tried to draw snowflakes, but with great difficulty; for before they could be drawn they would vanish from sight. More recently, photography has been employed to portray them in their evanescent form. W. A. Bentley of Jericho, Vermont, seems to have been the pioneer photomicrographer of snow crystals. He secured his first photomicrograph in 1885 and continued the work until he had 4,800 of them, with no two alike. Such photography reveals several things about the snowflake, which in turn reveal to us its spiritual revelations of the Holy Spirit and his ministry.

The snowflake ranges from 1/100 to 1/2 inch in size, and according to the testimony of science no two are found to be of the same design. God never makes two things exactly alike. Nothing in his creation is exactly like another. This means variety *ad infinitum*. Is not this a beautiful and needed instruction in regard to the work of the Holy Spirit? So many people seem to feel that others should receive the ministry of the Spirit in a way exactly similar to their reception of him. Many feel that there must be the same manifestation as a result of the Spirit's reception; and yet when we realize that God has not made any two personalities exactly alike, we are forced to realize that God does not approach any two personalities in the same way. Christ is the same, and the gospel is the same, and the ultimate result is the same; for while there are no two snowflakes alike, yet each is an individual snowflake, even though of different design. Each one receiving the Holy Spirit is a reborn soul, even though the design is different.

In other words, too many Christians expect others to have the same experience as they; but there must be variety in God's world. There will be variety of approach by which an individual is reached for Christ and to whom the Holy Spirit comes. One personality will be touched by one man's preaching, and another by another's. One person will be more impressed by another's habits or personality, while another will hold no attractiveness whatsoever. Oh, that earnest Christians might learn the truth of this variety in the Spirit's working! For oftentimes they do harm by trying to force a blueprint of their own on someone else, to whom it would make no appeal.

For this reason the Holy Spirit must lead in the work of soul-winning, and people must be very guarded and make sure that they are led of the Spirit before they approach another. Each human personality is more sacred than all else in the world to the Heavenly Father. It has been created in his likeness and image, and yet with variety of design. Let us, then, recognize this and allow God to employ his own means and develop his own design. Be willing to be used.

As there is variety in the snow, there is also beauty. Beauty of outline and richness of interior of the crystals are so great as to have attracted the attention and admiration of all students of the snow from earliest times. They far transcend in beauty, diversity, and perfect symmetry the crystals of any mineral substance.

> *White petals from the flowers that grow*
> *in the cold atmosphere.*
> *These starry blossoms, pure and white,*
> *Soft falling, falling, through the night,*
> *Have draped the woods and mere.*
> —Bungay, "The Artists of the Air."

Anyone who has seen a snowflake on a windowpane before it evanesces and disappears has seen the beauty of the lace-like design and marveled at the handiwork of God. Each snowflake is individual and has a unique and individual beauty of its own. Every believer is individual, and through the Holy Spirit may have a unique and individual beauty of his own.

The Holy Spirit seeks to make each beautiful in the likeness of Christ. Paul tells us that we have been "created in Christ Jesus unto good works, which God hath before ordained that we should walk in them." As we have shown before, the word for "good works" means "symphony," or in the Latin *poema*. A poem is a thing of artistry and beauty in symphony. Thus the Spirit will make us to be creations of perfect beauty, a symphony of God, or his poem. A poem has meter and rhythm, and expresses in most picturesque language the thing to be described. So the Christian filled with the Holy Spirit will reveal in language no words could express the beauty and majesty of Jesus Christ.

We have intimated before that the snow is evanescent. Evanescence is the act, fact, or quality of disappearing or fading gradually. This the snow is forced to do by the laws of nature. When it falls upon the windowpane, the heat from the inside gradually dissolves the design, and it melts away into a drop of moisture. Perhaps in this quality of the snow there comes one of the greatest blessings that we can ever learn in regard to the ministry of the Holy Spirit. It is the Holy Spirit within who makes it possible for us to be evanescent in Christ.

It was John the Baptist who when challenged by his disciples that others were following Jesus Christ, the One whom he had baptized in the waters of Jordan, was able to say, "He must increase, but I must decrease" (John 3:30). This is true. It was Paul who said "that in all things he might have the preeminence" (Col. 1:18). We must learn this secret of allowing self to evanesce in Christ.

In Forest Lawn Cemetery in Los Angeles there is a beautiful stained glass replica of da Vinci's "Last Supper." This was produced by the members of his family, and shipped from Italy to California. It is one of the most beautiful that I have ever seen. It has been placed in the great mausoleum in the cemetery in such a position that the light shines on it in a very remarkable way. An arrangement has been made whereby shutters, working electrically, gradually shut off the entire picture. As this is done, the picture fades from the two ends so that the faces of the disciples and their bodies nearest the end fade from the picture first. This continues gradually until the last form showing is that of Christ. And then the picture gradually fades and fades until at last his face alone is seen, and then gradually that fades.

Then the shutters reverse and the same process begins to work out again, only from the reverse angle. This time it is the face of Christ which appears first, and those of the disciples last. To me this beautifully reveals spiritual evanescence as it is illustrated to us in the snow. All the disciples fade away, until the face of Christ alone is seen. Truly, "he must increase, but I must decrease." This must be the prayer and aim of every true Christian. This is not the destruction of human personality, but rather the enhancing and enlargement thereof, as our life coalesces in and with the Holy Spirit, and gradually merges into the beauty and likeness of Jesus Christ.

Symbols of the Holy Spirit

NONE OF SELF
Oh, the bitter pain and sorrow
That a time could ever be
When I proudly said to Jesus,
"All of self, and none of thee."

Yet he found me; I beheld him
Bleeding on th' accursed tree;
And my wistful heart said, faintly,
"Some of self, and some of thee."

Day by day, his tender mercy,
Healing, helping, full and free,
Brought me lower, while I whispered,
"Less of self, and more of thee!"

Higher than the highest heavens,
Deeper than the deepest sea,
"Lord, thy love at last has conquered;
NONE of self and all of thee!"

In God's museum there is still another lesson we would learn from the snow, and that is that every design is perfect when it is the finished product of God. There is perfect symmetry, there is geometrical perfection in every snowflake. One never finds a snowflake coming from the hand of God unfinished or imperfect.

This is what the Holy Spirit has done and is seeking to do for us. Positionally, every believer is perfect in Jesus Christ. "Ye are complete in him" (Col. 2:10). But beyond the positional relationship there is that which is experiential, or a progressive sanctification in the Spirit of God as he is daily producing in us the gradual outworking of the perfectness of Christ. "All of us, as with unveiled faces we mirror the glory of the Lord, are transformed into the same likeness, from glory to glory, even as derived from the Lord the Spirit" (Weymouth, 2 Cor. 3:18). As with the snowflake there is individual perfectness and beauty, so it may be with us now and in the future, for we are to be like him in his glory.

Surely all of us will tread softly as we walk through God's museum, the snowstorm, and see again the individual treasures of his artistry as he deposits them upon the earth. These little

86

How Deep the Snow!

snowflakes are seeking to speak to us of the graciousness of God in the goodness of his gift to us of his own Holy Spirit.

The Immaculate Whiteness

White signifies regeneration in the Scripture. Isaiah, pleading with sin-sick Israel, says: "Come now, and let us reason together, saith the Lord: though your sins be as scarlet, they shall be as white as snow" (Isa. 1:18). By the regenerating power of the Spirit of God, we who were sinful and scarlet have been washed that we might be as the immaculate whiteness of the freshly-driven snow.

Paul declares: "But ye are washed, but ye are sanctified, but ye are justified in the name of the Lord Jesus, and by the Spirit of our God" (1 Cor. 6:11). He does not say that we are to be, but that we have been. It is a past, completed act; for the blood of Jesus Christ atones for, and the Spirit washes, each one who believes. We are washed, sanctified, and justified in the name of the Lord Jesus, but by the Spirit himself. Thus we see that Isaiah's reference to the whiteness of the snow in regeneration is really relating to the work of the Holy Spirit as he produces this condition in our lives.

In the most beautiful portrait we have of Jesus Christ, recorded for us by the Spirit of God himself in the first chapter of the Book of the Revelation, we read in part: "His head was white as wool, as white as snow." Taking this description with that given to us on the Mount of Transfiguration, where we read that he "was transfigured before them: and his face did shine as the sun, and his raiment was white as the light" (Matt. 17:2), we see that there is the immaculate whiteness of his glory. Snow and wool describe the whiteness of regeneration according to Isaiah, but they also describe the whiteness of his glory as he is depicted in John's description. But this is not only his glory; it is a picture of the glory that shall be ours. We too shall have raiment white as the light, and our face shall shine as the sun. The snow in its whiteness seeks to reveal to us the immaculate whiteness that is ours in regeneration now, and which will be ours in the body when his glory is received.

As these words are being written, the harbingers of winter are all around. There is less sunshine; there are longer nights, wintry blasts, occasional flakes of snow, heralding perhaps a snowstorm tomorrow. How fitting that as these things of nature are all about us we should say, "How deep the snow!" When it comes, let us remember the words of Jehovah to Job: "Hast thou entered into the treasures of the snow?" You may enjoy this message, but not enjoy the snow, because of the inconvenience which it causes to travel, and because of the added work of shoveling paths, with all of which one can readily agree. And yet perhaps if, when it comes, we will think how God is seeking to reveal himself in the ministry of his Holy Spirit through this phenomenon of nature, it will give added strength and courage for the day.

Let us remember again that snow and the Spirit both are the gifts of God. There is the region of both the snow and the Spirit, and the altitude above which there are the perennial snow fields, not only in nature but in the Spirit's blessing. Snow has become the poor man's gift from God, and in it we find the artistry of heaven. All these things are symbolical, suggestive, illustrative, revealing as we discover by analogy the Person and ministry of the Holy Spirit. Once again nature reveals the hand of God. "Hast thou entered into the treasures of the snow?" "The silent falling of the snow is to me one of the most solemn things in nature" (Longfellow).

So comes the silent working of the Spirit of God. How deep the snow! How full the Spirit!

THE SALT OF   7
THE EARTH

"Ye are the salt of the earth: but if the salt have lost his savor, wherewith shall it be salted? it is thenceforth good for nothing, but to be cast out, and to be trodden under foot of men." (Matthew 5:13)

As we approach the study of salt and its relationship or significance to the believer, we are dealing with a substance that is of great importance. Salt is one of the most important elements to the seasoning of food. Food is not palatable unless it has been properly seasoned.

In our day certain dietary practices have become a fad, or the justified prescription of medical science. Because of this, food served in restaurants and public eating places is sometimes cooked without the usual seasoning by the adding of certain condiments, such as salt. When we taste it, we find that it is almost tasteless, and it is necessary to add the seasoning ourselves. Salt has been eliminated from the diet of a great many people, and yet we know that food cannot be properly seasoned in this way. A good cook uses salt in the cooking, and the seasoning is at least partially done during that process. Long ago Eliphaz, speaking to Job, said: "Can that which is unsavory be eaten without salt? or is there any taste in the white of an egg?" (Job 6:6). In his day it was essential to palatable food, as it is in our day, but perhaps not so much avoided, because the occasional necessity of eliminating it from the diet was not recognized.

Symbols of the Holy Spirit

It will be interesting to discover the importance of salt in ancient history and in religious symbolism. Salt must have been quite unattainable by primitive man in many parts of the world. The *Odyssey* speaks of inlanders who did not know the sea and used no salt with their food. In some parts of our own country, and even of India (among the Todas), salt was first introduced by Europeans; and there are still parts of central Africa where it is a luxury available only to the rich.

Salt was usually associated with religious offerings (which consisted in whole or in part of cereal elements) and, we know from the Bible, also with the meat offerings. This practice obtained among Semitic peoples, and also among the Greeks and the Romans. Salt was referred to in the making of religious covenants and covenants of other types, probably because its preservative qualities became a fitting symbol of an enduring contract. Thus this particular element was used as that which sealed an obligation to fidelity.

In the parabolical teaching of Jesus, and especially in the Sermon on the Mount, we hear him referring to the believer as "the salt of the earth." The Sermon on the Mount has rightly been called the Manifesto of the Kingdom. Oftentimes people have misunderstood the meaning of this manifesto, and have sought to apply it to those who are unregenerate. While from an ethical standpoint it is the paramount teaching, yet without the indwelling and power of the Spirit of God, this ethic is impossible of attainment. Dr. G. Campbell Morgan, in his book *The Parables and Metaphors of Our Lord*, has this to say in regard to the Sermon on the Mount:

> *The manifesto is the ultimate code of laws for the Kingdom of God established upon the earth. . . . The function of the subjects of His Kingdom are so to live that they give goodness its opportunity and hold in check the force of corruption.*
>
> *Our Lord emphasized this with those words of satire, gentle, but clear and sharp as the lightning: "If the salt have lost his savor, wherewith shall it be salted?" I like the Scotch rendering of that: "If the salt has lost*

90

The Salt of the Earth

*its tang." That is a great word, tang, the pungent
power of salt. Jesus says His people are to exercise that
influence in the world. That is our responsibility,
though men may not be pleased* (p. 19).

There are some who hold what we might call an ultradispensa-
tional view, that the Sermon on the Mount is for the Jew in his
Kingdom relationship and for the Kingdom in the days of its estab-
lishment, but not for the Christian. While there is no question
whether Matthew is written with a strong Jewish emphasis, and
that its message has to do oftentimes with the relationship of the
Jew and the Kingdom, and *in* the Kingdom, we cannot accept the
view that it excludes all believers of our day. Therefore, when
Jesus says, "Ye are the salt of the earth," he is speaking to each
of us; for we are the children of the Kingdom. This is true because
of the fact that Paul tells us we have been delivered "from the
power of darkness, and (he) hath translated us into the kingdom of
his dear Son" (Col. 1:13). And while this Kingdom is not universal
or physical, yet it is spiritual and the Kingdom of God, of which
we are citizens; and it is the sum total of all the redemptive work
of Jesus Christ, whether in this dispensation or in any other.

The Sermon on the Mount applies to us because "all scripture is
given by inspiration of God, and is profitable for doctrine, for
reproof, for correction, for instruction in righteousness: that the
man of God may be perfect, thoroughly furnished unto all good
works" (2 Tim. 3:16, 17). All interpreters seem willing to appro-
priate the "blesseds" in the Sermon on the Mount. But fair
exegesis or treatment of the Scriptures does not exclude a portion
of some passages and accept the balance. This is the thing that
modernists and liberals are doing in their treatment of the Word
of God; and we who hold to the Word as infallible must be as fair
as we want them to be.

Therefore, as citizens of his Kingdom, the Manifesto is for us;
and we as believers must be seasoned with salt. "Ye are the salt of
the earth; but if the salt has lost his savor, wherewith shall it be
salted?" Dr. Morgan suggests his own liking for the Scotch translation, which reads: "If the salt has lost its tang." This is ex-
pressive and pungent in its meaning. Thus we shall seek to discover

91

the ministry of the Holy Spirit as he produces this tang in the life of the believer.

Saline Productivity of the Holy Spirit

Dr. Morgan reminds us that salt *per se* is absolutely pure. His statement is, "Salt is not antiseptic, but aseptic." "Antiseptic" is something which is against poison, and which tends to its cure. "Aseptic" is something which is devoid of poison in itself. As salt is pure in itself, so also, through the indwelling of the Spirit of God, is the believer. There is first of all a positional relationship of righteousness in Christ. "He hath made him to be sin for us, who knew no sin; that we might be made the righteousness of God in him" (2 Cor. 5:21).

In other words, in Christ every believer has received the divine nature, and in the divine nature has received the righteousness which is of God. "Whosoever is born of God doth not commit sin; for his seed remaineth in him: and he cannot sin, because he is born of God" (1 John 3:9). Is not this the seed referred to by Peter as the divine nature, and the seed given in the new birth which all believers have received? It is this nature which cannot sin, and in this nature we have this positional relationship. Paul tells us that our "life is hid with Christ in God" (Col. 3:3).

The story is told of a father and a son watching the changing of the Horse Guards at St. James's Palace, London. The boy remarked to his father concerning the beautiful white coats worn by the soldiers; but the coats were red, and the father so informed the boy. However, the boy could not be convinced. The father was beginning to wonder whether the child was color-blind, and he had never known it; but before he raised the question, he thought it would be wise to look at the soldiers from the same point of vantage as his son. Leaning down to the level of his son's eyes, he observed that, strangely, the red uniforms had been transformed to white. Wondering why this was, he discovered that the boy had been looking through a red stained-glass border. As he looked at red through red it became white.

In the physical language that we use to try to describe the things of the Spirit, we may say that as God looks at the red of our sinful life through the red of the precious blood of his own Son, atonement is made and he sees our sinful condition in the white purity of the sinlessness of his own Son.

> *Pure, so pure in the sight of God,*
> *Purer I could not be;*
> *For in the Person of his Son*
> *I'm just as pure as he.*

Not only is there the positional relationship in righteousness, but there is the possibility of a progressive righteousness through the power and presence of the Spirit of God. As we have seen before, the divine nature comes with the reception of the Holy Spirit. We are born of the Spirit unto his purity, but we are empowered of the Spirit into his purity, that we may be ever-growing in the grace and knowledge of our Lord, that we may be without guile, and that through the progressive sanctifying power of the Spirit of God we may grow daily into his image and likeness.

Now we must seek to discover the reaction of salt in its relationship to corruption, for we know that that is one of its functions in the physical sense. Quoting again from Dr. Morgan, we read:

> *Salt never cures corruption. It prevents the spread of corruption. If meat is tainted and corrupt, salt will not make it untainted and pure. But salt in its neighborhood will prevent the spread of corruption to that which otherwise would become tainted. The figure is that of a moral quality operating on the earth level, amongst men living in the midst of material things, preventing the spread of corruption. The impurity of an evil man cannot be cured by a good man working at his side in an office; but the things the good man will not do and the things he will not say will give the boy in the same office a chance, because it will check the evil man. Salt is aseptic.*

Then follows the reminder of the citizen's duty in the Kingdom:

> *The function of the subjects of His Kingdom is to live in the midst of humanity in the terrible condition of*

> *sin, and by living there according to the ethic of the*
> *Kingdom of God, to prevent the spread of evil. It is the*
> *Lord's work to cure it, thank God. However impure*
> *and corrupt the heart may be, He can cleanse it, and*
> *make it purer than the driven snow. The subjects of*
> *His Kingdom are so to live that they give goodness its*
> *opportunity and hold in check the forces of corruption*
> (pp. 18, 19).

It is only by the presence of the Holy Spirit in our life that this saline condition is made possible, and the good has its real opportunity. Paul says: "The manifestation [working] of the Spirit is given to every man to profit withal" (1 Cor. 12:7). He is God's gift to the believer, by which we may profit in the things of the Spirit. It is the continuing presence of the Holy Spirit as salt in the believer that hinders the power of evil and the spread of corruption.

Some expositors believe that the reference in 2 Thessalonians 2:7, "For the mystery of iniquity doth already work: only he who now letteth [hindereth] will let, until he be taken out of the way," is to the Holy Spirit in the believer, remaining in him, hindering the forces of evil, until he be taken out, either through death or the coming of Christ. There are others who do not so interpret this Scripture; but at least it is most suggestive of the thing we are trying to say. The believer as salt is a hindrance to corruption, and the salt, being aseptic or pure, symbolizing the Holy Spirit in his purity, allows goodness, the goodness of God, to do its work.

A Reiteration of the Ministry of the Spirit and the Kingdom Witness

Once again let us remind ourselves of the relevance of the Kingdom; and it would be wise for the reader to turn back and read again the words of Dr. Morgan on the Manifesto of the Kingdom. We discover that Jesus spoke these words to his own disciples. "And seeing the multitudes, he went up into a mountain: and when he was set, his disciples came unto him: and he opened his mouth, and taught them" (Matt. 5:1, 2). Thus we cannot escape its relationship to us as believers and the spiritual implications which it

The Salt of the Earth

places upon us in the realm of ethics and behavior.

The citizen's function in an evil age is to be as salt. "Ye are the salt of the earth." As citizens of the Kingdom, we are to live in such a way that we give goodness, which is the Christ-nature within, the opportunity to do good and hold in check the forces of evil. This is for the individual believer, but it is also for the entire body of Christ. Both individually and corporately, we are the salt of the earth.

Remembering the use of the Scottish word "tang" instead of "savor" by Dr. Morgan, we would do well to remind ourselves that the tang in the salt of life is given by the Holy Spirit. It is possible for the salt to lose its tang or savor. The best explanation seems to me to be that in the oriental system of taxation, high imports on salt were seldom lacking and were often carried out oppressively, with the result that smuggled salt was apt to reach the consumer in an impure state, having been largely mixed with earth. Thus, "the salt which has lost its savor" is simply the earthly residuum of such an impure salt after the sodium chloride has been washed out. Another has suggested, "The impure salt of Syria, when exposed to rain or sun, or stored in damp houses, is apt to lose its taste and become useless" (Davis's *Bible Dictionary*).

In comparison we see that we as believers, like salt, may lose our tang through an impure mixture with the earth. Paul says, "Come out from among them, and be ye separate" (2 Cor. 6:17). That there is a true spiritual separation cannot be denied. Frankly, we oftentimes feel that people have been inconsistent in regard to this separation and have assumed certain attitudes which are not justified by Scripture, and ignored those that are. God has always abhorred a mixture. The Decalogue definitely prohibits the sharing of devotional worship between God and idols, or false gods. His instruction to the children of Israel was as follows:

> *Thou shalt not sow thy vineyard with divers seeds: lest the fruit of thy seed which thou hast sown, and the fruit of thy vineyard, be defiled. Thou shalt not plow with an ox and an ass together. Thou shalt not wear a garment of divers sorts, as of woolen and linen to-*

gether. Thou shalt make thee fringes upon the four quarters of thy vesture, wherewith thou coverest thyself (Deut. 22:9-12).

Perhaps we have lost tang in our life because we have too much of that which is earthy or carnal. Let each one search out his own life, not the life of others, and be determined of his own need.

Salt also loses its savor when it is exposed or stored in a damp house. Our body is the house of the Spirit, but if it is damp and dark spiritually, the Spirit of God cannot produce salinity and the blessings therein. Again, let us remember that this is both individual and corporate. The individual believer today has very much lost the tang of the Spirit in his life, and the church is preeminently cold and barren because of this missing element.

As salt may lose its tang, it may also keep it; and we have the promise that the Holy Spirit has come to abide with us and be in us forever. Therefore, it is not his fault but rather ours if our life is no longer seasoned with salt. Paul taught in another figure the secret of such a needed condition. "Be not drunk with wine, wherein is excess; but be filled with the Spirit" (Eph. 5:18). To be filled is so simple we stumble over it. In the law of nature, if we would fill a vessel with some element we must first empty out the element that is occupying it. If the vessel is filled with water and we would fill it with milk, the water must first be poured out and then the milk poured in. If the vessel is simply filled with air, the element itself will force the air out as it is poured in. Our life is but a vessel, and if it is empty, then the Spirit of God can fill it. He has no other alternative, and by his complete infilling our life will find the saline qualities of the Spirit of God.

The Scriptural Implications of the Purposes of Salt and the Spirit's Counterpart

There are many instances where salt has been used in Scripture, and we shall seek to draw the spiritual parallels from these uses.

Salt was used to strengthen newborn babes. "Son of man, cause Jerusalem to know her abominations... And as for thy nativity, in the day thou wast born... thou wast not salted at all" (Ezek.

The Salt of the Earth

16:2, 4). The Spirit of God is speaking through the prophet to the people of Jerusalem, who were in a condition of spiritual weakness. It must have been a custom in that day to use salt for the strengthening of the newborn child. Apparently a salt solution was used in postnatal care. Israel was like a foundling, with no one to give care at birth.

So many of us need strengthening as newborn babes. We are as foundlings cast out upon the world; but not so often for we have been given the Holy Spirit. As the newborn babe was washed with salt for strengthening, so the newborn babe in Christ is "washed with pure water" (Heb. 10:22). Water in the Word of God, as we shall discover in another message, is symbolical of the Holy Spirit. Therefore, when the writer of the Epistle to the Hebrews says that we have had "our bodies washed with pure water," he is simply saying that we have been washed with the saline solution of the Spirit of God.

As we saw at the beginning of our message, salt is absolutely essential to the proper seasoning of food. "Can that which is unsavory be eaten without salt?" (Job 6:6). As we observed, many have been placed on diets in our day and must eat such unseasoned and tasteless food. But we are trying to show that as salt seasons the food that we eat, so the Holy Spirit seasons the food of life. How unsavory this food of life, the Word of God, often described as dry as dust and tasteless! And it is, until the Holy Spirit comes in that he may season it and make it palatable to the believer! When he comes, through his divine revelation and instruction the Word of God becomes interesting and edifying.

I remember an elderly lady in one of my pastorates who, as we members of the church read the Bible together during the course of the year, told of her experience when she came to the genealogies of Genesis 5. She said that they were so uninteresting that she took them all in one gulp, just as she ate her spinach. I am afraid that many Christians so devour the Word of God because they have not the seasoning of the Spirit. When the Holy Spirit comes, he can season even the genealogies, for the promise is: "He will guide you into all truth" (John 16:13).

If the Bible has been uninteresting to you, try a little of the salt of the Holy Spirit, and you will find it no longer unsavory but the most delicious spiritual food that you have ever eaten. The prophet saw a scroll and was ordered to eat it, and as he ate it he found it sweet to his taste. So the Word of God will be to you.

We want also to observe that the Holy Spirit alone can give the salt of grace in our life, in a spiritual sacrifice or offering. Recall if you will that the suggestion was made in the beginning that salt was used by ancient peoples in their sacrifices and in the making of covenants. God's instruction to Moses was: "Every oblation of thy meat offering shalt thou season with salt; neither shalt thou suffer the salt of the covenant of thy God to be lacking from thy meat offering: with all thine offerings thou shalt offer salt" (Lev. 2:13). God made salt essential to every meat offering, not just that it might be properly seasoned, but also that the spiritual significance might be manifest.

The sacerdotal worship of the Old Testament has given place to the spiritual worship of the New. Paul makes this clear in Romans 12:1: "I plead with you therefore, brethren, by the compassion of God, to present all your faculties to him as a living and holy sacrifice, acceptable to him—a spiritual mode of worship" (Weymouth). Thus we see that the believer's sacrifice or worship is not in the offering of a slain victim, or in the preparing of the meal for an offering, but in the presentation of life. We believe that the burning of candles, the offering of incense, and all these other things are foreign to the dispensation in which we live, which is primarily one of the presence and superintendency of the Holy Spirit. Through his indwelling, we are to offer our lives unto God as our spiritual mode of worship. As the meat offering had to be seasoned with salt, so the offering of our life must be seasoned with the salt of grace. In other words, we cannot be an offense unto him or unto our fellowmen.

Jesus uttered strong words when he said: "Whoso shall offend one of these little ones which believe in me, it were better for him that a millstone were hanged about his neck, and that he were drowned in the depth of the sea" (Matt. 18:6). "Every one shall be salted with fire, and every sacrifice shall be salted with salt. Salt is good: but if the salt have lost his saltness, wherewith will ye season it? [the *it* refers to the sacrifice as its antecedent] Have salt in yourselves, and have peace one with another" (Mark 9:49, 50). The punishment is severe for those who become an offense; but one need not become an offense when the salt of the Spirit and his grace is in the life. Then will we be at peace one with the other.

How useless is the offering of self merely as a self act without the enablement of the Spirit of God! The words of Samuel to Saul in the day of his disobedience, and the uncovering of that disobedience by the lowing of the oxen and the bleating of the sheep, when God had commanded, "Go and smite Amalek, and utterly destroy all that they have" (1 Sam. 15:3), were not upset by Saul's alibi. Samuel's word was, "To obey is better than sacrifice, and to hearken than the fat of rams" (1 Sam. 15:22). This is still the practice God demands.

The speech of the believer often betrays him; and yet, when our speech is seasoned by the grace of the Holy Spirit, there will be no betrayal. "Let your speech be always with grace, seasoned with salt, that ye may know how ye ought to answer every man" (Col. 4:6). I believe that the example of Jesus would be well heeded. "All bare him witness, and wondered at the gracious words which proceeded out of his mouth" (Lk. 4:22). This is the record of the people as Jesus returned to his hometown, Nazareth, to bear witness to himself and his ministry in the synagogue of his boyhood. When our speech is seasoned with salt, the salt of the Holy Spirit, all will bear witness of us and wonder at the gracious words which proceed out of our mouth.

Christ is more often dishonored by the corrupt conversation, the impure and unchristian words which fall from the lips of the believer than in almost any other way. If we could have the divine guarantee that such sin and disobedience will not be found in our life, it can be only when we have allowed the Spirit of God to take control of heart and tongue. Thus will he season with the salt of his grace every word which we utter.

The Irrevocability of the Covenant of Salt

As we have seen, salt was used in covenants, not only among the Semitics, but also among the Greek and Roman peoples. It was thus used because its preservative qualities made it a fitting symbol of an enduring contract, and this particular element was used as that which sealed an obligation to fidelity.

Aaron was instructed that the Levites were to receive the heave offering for their compensation. Of all the tribes, they were given no inheritance; but God said that he himself would be their inheritance. In the instructions given to Aaron, we read: "All the heave offerings of the holy things, which the children of Israel offer unto the Lord, have I given thee, and thy sons and thy daughters with thee, by a statute for ever: it is a covenant of salt for ever before the Lord unto thee and to thy seed with thee" (Num. 18:19). God says it is a covenant of salt forever, for the Lord and unto thee and thy seed forever. Salt was used in order that its preservative qualities might show it to be an enduring covenant, and also that it might be sealed with the obligation of fidelity. This is an unconditional covenant, based upon the salt of God's faithfulness. It could never be revoked.

So in our spiritual comparison we find the irrevocable covenant of the Spirit. Paul tells the believer that he is "blessed . . . with all spiritual blessings in heavenly places" (Eph. 1:3). This is not a partial blessing, but a complete blessing, made by the irrevocable gift and indwelling of the Holy Spirit. "I will pray the Father, and he shall give you another Comforter [Paraclete], that he may abide with you for ever" (John 14:16). Again we compare this statement of Jesus as to the enduring presence of the Spirit with the word of John: "His seed remaineth in him" (1 John 3:9). The seed of Jesus Christ is the Holy Spirit, given to us in the new birth and regeneration.

Salt of the covenant, showing it to be enduring, unconditional, and irrevocable, is in the Person of the Holy Spirit. He is not the symbol of fidelity and preservation, like salt; he *is* the fidelity and preservation itself. Thus, believer, you may rest in the assurance that the covenant of God's grace, in which he has given to you his own divine Spirit, is without repentance. God will not recall him from your presence; but you must realize that while he may be with you, he may be made comparatively impotent because you have not been willing to surrender your life to him.

As a brief résumé, let us rediscover that the Holy Spirit is the

The Salt of the Earth

saline deposit in every believer. "Ye are the salt of the earth." The believer is God's salt box. This was simply the box in which the salt was kept, similar to the barrel in which our mothers used to keep the flour. We are the repository in which God has placed the salt of his Spirit that the earth might be salted. God grant that the tang may be ever present in our life, and to this end may our life be strengthened, seasoned, and of fragrant, graceful speech, lest we lose the tang and the salt lose its savor.

Our life is a spiritual condiment; we may, by our good seasoning, season those with whom we come in contact. This should be the primary aim of our life, that others may be helped and that corruption may be arrested, and the forces of evil and the author of evil may be hindered in their purpose. Remember, the Sermon on the Mount is the Manifesto of the Kingdom; we are citizens of the Kingdom of the Son of God's love, and as such we must be seasoned with salt, that the spiritual food which we dispense to the world about us may not be unsavory and unpalatable.

> *Ye are the salt of the earth: but if the salt have lost his savor, wherewith shall it be salted? it is thenceforth good for nothing, but to be cast out, and to be trodden under foot of men* (Matt. 5:13).

SEALED WITH HIS SIGNET

"In whom ye also trusted, after that ye heard the word of truth, the gospel of your salvation: in whom also, after that ye believed, ye were sealed with that Holy Spirit of promise." (Ephesians 1:13)

The preparation of this chapter finds me in a happy transition, for most of the previous messages have been in the realm of science, with which I have not had much personal acquaintance or firsthand knowledge. Mine is not a scientific mind, nor has my training been along that line; and it has been necessary to spend many hours in research, as I have sought to cull the information which the scientist would give.

However, this message is in the realm with which I am acquainted and in which I am trained, that of law and business; and it is more to my liking. When one begins to talk about seals, the earnest, acceptance, and other things, there is an immediate understanding so far as the preacher is concerned.

One of the figures of speech used in Scripture to denote the Person and ministry of the Holy Spirit is that of the seal; and thus we shall consider the royal signet of the King, which we believe to be the Holy Spirit, and the earnest or consideration of our redemption. The basis for our study is the word of Paul: "In whom ye also trusted, after that ye heard the word of truth, the gospel of your salvation: in whom also, after that ye believed, ye were sealed with that Holy Spirit of promise, which is the earnest of our inheritance until the redemption of the purchased possession, unto the praise of his glory" (Eph. 1:13, 14). This reveals to us the Holy Spirit's ministry in a sealed and finished transaction. It is the justification of words we often sing, " 'Tis done, the great transaction's done." We would discover the meaning of the seal and of the earnest in order to appreciate more deeply the Holy Spirit's presence and power and purpose in our life.

Sealed with His Signet

When one considers a seal, the first question is to discover the owner or the one whose imprint is on the seal. It was King Ahasuerus who, at the behest of Haman, caused the decree to be written for the slaying of the Jews: "There was written according to all that Haman had commanded ... to every people after their language; in the name of king Ahasuerus was it written, and sealed with the king's ring" (Esth. 3:12). It was the king's ring with the king's seal that made the decree effective.

The same was true in the experience of Daniel, when cast into the den of lions. "A stone was brought, and laid upon the mouth of the den; and the king sealed it with his own signet" (Dan. 6:17). While they are not types of God or of his Son Jesus Christ in their possession and exercise of authority, these kings do show with the seal that there must always be the one who seals.

With us, it is the Heavenly Father who seals, he having first sealed Jesus of Nazareth as his own Son. "Him hath God the Father sealed" (John 6:27). This probably is a reference to the time of his baptism, when we find the Trinity present. It was the Father who spoke, saying, "This is my beloved Son, in whom I am well pleased" (Matt. 3:17). It was the Holy Spirit who came in the form of a dove and rested upon him; it was the Son in the waters of baptism who was being identified and, in the words of John, sealed with the Holy Spirit. He was being sealed, not for security as with the believer, but for identification as the Son of God.

But the believer has also been sealed, as we have discovered from our text. The Authorized Version says: "In whom also, after that ye believed, ye were sealed with that Holy Spirit." A better

103

translation is: "When you believed, you were sealed with the Holy Spirit." We believe that simultaneously with believing faith comes salvation, and with salvation, which of course means regeneration, the sealing and incoming of the Holy Spirit.

Having discovered that it is God the Father who seals, we now determine if possible the meaning of the seal. With Ahasuerus it was the king's personal signet: and with God, we believe it is the Father's personal seal, or heaven's royal signet. This is not some emotional experience, but the Person of the Holy Spirit himself as he comes to indwell the believer. The Word says: "God, who hath also given unto us his Holy Spirit"(1 Thess. 4:8). We believe in the holy Trinity, and that the Holy Spirit is the third person thereof. He himself is very God of very God, one with the Father and one with the Son, a divine personality, coming to us individually as a personality, in all his fullness.

A personality cannot be segregated or separated from its component parts. When any of us enter a certain place, we enter in the completeness of our individual personality, even though perhaps that personality may not be fully active at that particular time. The seal of the Father or his holy signet is none other than the Spirit of God himself.

Now we must discover who are the sealed. Paul says "ye," and he was addressing his epistle both "to the saints which are at Ephesus, and to the faithful in Christ Jesus" (Eph. 1:1). This is not for just the few who would designate themselves faithful, but for all those who have exercised believing faith, and thus have full faith or faith-fullness, through the grace of our Lord Jesus Christ. As sinners we are redeemed or regenerated by him. By the indwelling of his divine Spirit we are sanctified and made saints; and in such sanctification the Spirit becomes the seal of God upon every believer. Jesus gave promise of this when he said: "Even the Spirit of truth; whom the world cannot receive, because it seeth him not, neither knoweth him: but ye know him; for he dwelleth with you, and shall be in you" (John 14:17). Again, let us emphatically say that the sealing with the Spirit is not for any particular class of believers, but for all, and that the seal is applied instantaneously when saving faith is exercised and salvation given.

Sealed with His Signet

The Meaning of the Seal

The seal in legal procedure or requirement is of very little importance today. It is used upon deeds transferring pieces of real estate, on the last will and testament of individuals, and sometimes in other transactions. However, with very few exceptions, possibly the transfer of real estate, a seal is not usually required. However, in Paul's time the seal was of great importance, as it was in all times covered in the period of Scripture. In that time, as it has even today, the seal had certain legal benefit.

The seal guaranteed the transaction. In law the seal was final as to a good and sufficient consideration, and no question could ever be raised in regard to this when once the seal had been affixed and the document signed. Jeremiah was instructed to buy a seal from his cousin, Hanameel. We read: "And I bought the field of Hanameel my uncle's son, that was in Anathoth, and weighed him the money, even seventeen shekels of silver. And I subscribed [signed] the evidence, and sealed it, and took witnesses, and weighed him the money in the balances" (Jer. 32:9, 10). This transaction could never be questioned; and the cousin could never say that Jeremiah had not paid a sufficient consideration. The matter was closed when once the instrument was subscribed and sealed before the witnesses.

This is symbolic of the fact that the seal of the Holy Spirit guarantees a good and sufficient consideration in the price Christ paid for our redemption and the value was received thereby. Redemption is a two-party contract, made between God the Father and God the Son, executed by the Holy Spirit as the witness for the seal, so that the consideration can never be questioned. We recall the tremendous price that was paid, for we know that we "were not redeemed with corruptible things, as silver and gold . . . but with the precious blood of Christ, as of a lamb without blemish and without spot" (1 Pet. 1:18, 19). Christ himself said: "The Son of man came not to be ministered unto, . . . but to give his life a ransom" (Mark 10:45). The price he paid was his own life. This price satisfied divine justice, the curse of a broken law, and can never be questioned.

In regard to the value given, we know that through the paying of this price the individual believer may be reconciled to God. The value received by the Son is his inheritance in the saints: "the riches of the glory of his inheritance in the saints" (Eph. 1:18). And we think of the words of Isaiah: "He shall see of the travail of his soul, and shall be satisfied" (Isa. 53:11). Never can the consideration for your redemption and mine be questioned. The seal of the Holy Spirit has become the eternal guarantee and makes impossible the questioning thereof.

The seal also identifies ownership. Many people in our day are concerned with the mark of the beast. "He causeth all, both small and great, rich and poor, free and bond, to receive a mark in their right hand, or in their foreheads: and that no man might buy or sell, save he that had the mark" (Rev. 13:16, 17). This is the mark that identifies the individual wearing it with the Antichrist, and makes possible the purchase of the necessities of life in a day of terrible economic boycott. But we are not concerned with the mark of the beast, but with the mark of God's ownership. The same Scriptures say: "They shall see his face; and his name shall be in their foreheads" (Rev. 22:4).

This is all in the future; but we have been sealed now, in order that God's ownership might be made known and we might be identified with those who are his. "When ye believed, ye were sealed." Ephesus in the days of Paul was a maritime city, and we are told that its harbor was the depository for the timber brought in from the nearby sections. Representatives of great companies would come, carefully separate and select the timber which they desired, make their purchase, apply the seal, then go away to forget about it until the time when it should be claimed. In that day it would be identified by the owner through his seal. The same practice is employed in the western part of our country, where the cattle are branded in order that ownership may be unquestioned. Sometimes thieves seek to re-brand or change the brand; but, thank God, thieves can never break through and change the brand that has been placed upon us in the seal of the Holy Spirit! When Christ comes, we shall be identified as his by the seal, or the presence of the Holy Spirit in our life. Jesus said: "He dwelleth with you, and shall be in you." We know that he can never depart, and thus the seal can never be taken away. It is through the permanency and eternal indwelling of the Holy Spirit in those who believe that we rest in the ownership of God.

Furthermore, the seal carries security. It was by a Roman seal that the attempt was made to secure the body of Jesus. When Daniel was placed in the den of lions, it was the king's seal which sealed the den. But in both instances the power of God was too great. The only seal that cannot be broken is the seal of God. The strongest earthly seals have been broken, as suggested in the resurrection of Jesus Christ, where the seal of the great Roman Empire meant nothing. Military dispatches are sent under the security of a seal, as are other important documents. The affixing of the seal on the outside, or to the lock, means that that which is within is not to be tampered with.

This is what the seal means in our life. God is saying to Satan, "Hands off! This child belongs to me." So long as the seal remains, the security is complete. The Holy Spirit is dwelling in us and will be with us forever. Therefore, we rest in the power of the Holy Spirit, in the strength of God, and in the security of his seal.

But the seal has another important function in that it leaves its imprint or facsimile in the wax. When King Ahasuerus allowed Haman to use his seal upon the decree that would destroy the Jews, Haman pressed the king's ring into the soft wax; and when it hardened, the imprint of the seal was there. This used to be the custom in the sealing of letters, and sometimes is today. How illustrative this is of the sealing of God! When the Holy Spirit seals us, it is when our heart is warm through the wooing of God's love and the realization of the fact that Christ died for us. The seal leaves the imprint of God's facsimile or life upon us, the likeness of his Son; and as the wax hardens, the likeness remains. He is the Spirit of life, of truth, of grace, of humility. The very imprint of Christ is made possible in our life by the indwelling of the Holy Spirit, producing in us the ninefold fruit of his own likeness. This is not through self-effort, but by the power of God.

The Reception of the Earnest

Paul speaks not only of the sealing, but also of the earnest: "Which is the earnest of our inheritance until the redemption of the purchased possession.'' Here the reference is to the Holy Spirit of promise.

The meaning of the earnest is ascertained from law. The earnest is a pledge, or part of something given or done in advance. Sometimes it is money or goods given to bind an agreement. It is an indication of what may be expected, the firstfruits or the foretaste. In olden times if one were to purchase a tract of land, the contracting parties would go to the land, an agreement would be entered into, part of the purchase price would be paid, and the buyer would take away a spadeful of the earth. This was his earnest. In other words, it was a pledge in kind of that which he was to receive at a later date in completeness. It was something for him to take home, to keep as an evidence of the purchased possession, by which he would prove or identify that which he had purchased.

The believer's earnest is the presence of the Holy Spirit in life; for he brings to us the firstfruits of our inheritance, or that which is in kind with the complete possession. In other words, we receive a little bit of heaven now as we become partakers of the divine nature. John says: "As he is, so are we in this world" (1 John 4:17). Is he the Son of God? We are sons of God in him. Is he the beloved of God? So are we in him. Is he the accepted of God? So are we in him. Is he the righteous one? So are we in him. Is he the crucified? So are we in him. Is he the Risen One? So are we in him. Is he the eternal One? So are we in him. And so we might continue in the revelation of the oneness of our relationship in Jesus Christ, that as he is so are we.

The consummation of the earnest pledge is in the day when the purchased possession is redeemed. Is not that just what Paul is saying—"until the redemption of the purchased possession"? We have been purchased; one day we will be redeemed. But until that day we have been pledged and sealed, we have received the earnest of our inheritance until the day of its claiming by the Owner, God the Father, for his Son, Jesus Christ. "Our conversation [citizenship] is in heaven; from whence also we look for the Saviour, the Lord Jesus Christ: who shall change our vile body, that it may be fashioned like unto his glorious body" (Phil. 3:20, 21).

Sealed with His Signet

This is the day in which we groan, and all creation groans, waiting for the redemption of the body. The body is the dwelling place of God the Holy Spirit, and this body has been sealed and made secure for God; and even though the spirit may leave the body, one day God will identify it as his own, and it will be raised in his likeness and glory. We are now the possessors of the earnest, and in that possession are partakers of the divine nature. The seal of God is upon us and cannot be broken. The consideration can never be questioned; and in that glad day when he comes, the identification will be complete.

According to law, the seal carried great import. But here is law in grace. The work of Jesus Christ on behalf of the believer can never be impeached. It has been done with finality. There are no errors or mistakes or failures in that which he has accomplished. How explicitly the Spirit of God interprets the means of our redemption! God takes the things by which man carries on his business and proves from them the things of eternity. We have been sealed of God for God.

This is not only the statement of divine law as recorded in the Scripture, but proven in the comparison we have made with the civil law. In the Book of the Revelation the 144,000 are sealed for God. Many claim that they belong to that particular set of the elect; but happy are those who know that, without any reference to this particular group, they have been sealed in the moment when they have believed! That is the election, and these are the elect of the day in which we now live. Blessed is the man or woman who knows the truth of the promise of Paul: "In whom ye also trusted, after that ye heard the word of truth, the gospel of your salvation; in whom also, after that ye believed, ye were sealed with the Holy Spirit of promise."

In the seal he has given evidence of security of ownership and of his likeness. In the earnest he has given to us the firstfruits, or the foretaste, that we may have enjoyment now and the pledge of the full inheritance later on.

O Blessed Paraclete,
Assert thine inward sway;

Symbols of the Holy Spirit

My body make the temple meet
For thy perpetual stay.

Too long this house of thine,
By alien loves possessed,
Has shut from thee its inner shrine,
Kept thee a slighted guest.

Now rend, O Spirit blest,
The veil of my poor heart;
Enter thy long forbidden rest,
And never more depart.

O to be filled with thee,
I ask not aught beside;
For all unholy guests must flee,
If thou in me abide.

THE RIDDLE   9
OF THE WINDS

"Then said he unto me, Prophesy unto the wind, prophesy, son of man, and say to the wind, Thus saith the Lord God; Come from the four winds, O breath, and breathe upon these slain, that they may live. So I prophesied as he commanded me, and the breath came into them, and they lived, and stood up upon their feet, an exceeding great army." (Ezekiel 37:9, 10)

I once heard a radio news commentator use the expression "the riddle of the winds" to describe how the winds had foiled the plans of the enemy. The aptness of these words as a title for this message immediately flashed through my mind. That the winds have often been an enigma to our enemy is a matter of history. On April 22, 1915, the Germans used poison gas for the first time. They did so because the report of their meteorologist assured them that the wind would be blowing away from their lines for a considerable period of time. However, this proved to be wrong and within a short time after the gas had been loosed, the wind changed and blew it back over their lines, destroying many of their own men.

Many accounts could be given of somewhat similar experiences, not of the use of gas, but of the enigma of the winds. The news commentator was not the first to suggest that the winds present a riddle. Almost 2,000 years ago Jesus said the same thing to Nicodemus: "The wind bloweth where it listeth, and thou hearest the sound thereof, but canst not tell whence it cometh, and whither it goeth: so is every one that is born of the Spirit'' (John 3:8). In his inability to understand the working of the Holy Spirit in the new birth, Nicodemus found himself face to face with another problem equally unexplainable, the problem presented by Jesus.

There are many like Nicodemus today. Although the reality of things is all about us, they refuse to believe because of their so-called scientific minds. They question the supernatural, as Nicodemus did, and say they cannot accept anything that is not possible of explanation. Some years ago I was talking with a doctor who said that he could not believe that man had a soul. Questioned as to his inability to believe, he said that he was scientific and could not believe things that could not be proven in the laboratory or that could not be measured or seen. He was quite adamant in his position, but when questioned as to whether he had ever been able to measure or see pain, which he readily admitted was a reality, he saw the fallacy of his position. Many doctors have missed their mark on even attempting a correct diagnosis of the cause which produces the pain.

No, there are too many things in the world which are real and yet cannot be seen, measured, or explained for any of us to take such a position against accepting the supernatural. Long ago, one of the wisest men who ever lived recorded these words: "As thou knowest not what is the way of the spirit, nor how the bones do grow in the womb of her that is with child: even so thou knowest not the works of God who maketh all'' (Eccl. 11:5).

As we have been seeking to prove from the objects studied just what is the peculiar ministry of the Holy Spirit as particularly demonstrated or illustrated in his various properties or peculiar relationships, so we would discover the spiritual analogy between the winds of the heaven and the winds of the Spirit, or the breath of God. In Ezekiel 37 we have the vision of the valley of dry bones. This is a prophecy primarily relating itself to the revival of Israel, which will have its complete fulfillment some day in the future. However, the prophecy in its spiritual sense is being fulfilled every day. The people of God in every age are as a valley of dry bones. They grow indifferent, they lag in service, they grow weak in testimony or witness and need reviving.

The Riddle of the Winds

In our text the analogy between the wind and the Spirit of God is made very clear. "Then said he unto me, Prophesy unto the wind, prophesy, son of man, and say to the wind, Thus saith the Lord God; Come from the four winds, O breath, and breathe upon these slain, that they may live." Ezekiel refers to the four winds as breaths. To determine the meaning thereof we go to the first use of this expression, showing that it in that instance, and thus in this, refers to the Holy Spirit. In the description of the creation of man we read: "And the Lord God formed man of the dust of the ground, and breathed into his nostrils the breath of life; and man became a living soul" (Gen. 2:7). We know that the breath which God breathed into the nostrils of Adam was the breath of his own Spirit. "In him was life" (John 1:4). Job confirms this view: "The Spirit of God hath made me, and the breath of the Almighty hath given me life" (Job 33:4). As the winds come from the four corners of the earth and breathe upon the slain of the vision, that they might live again, so the winds of the Spirit or the breath of God comes upon the dry bones of the believer and the Church, that they might be revived.

We shall seek to learn the secret of a Spirit-controlled life in the school of the winds, and to discover that the prophecy can be fulfilled in each life. "So I prophesied as he commanded me, and the breath came into them, and they lived, and stood up upon their feet, an exceeding great army" (Ezek. 37:10).

BREATHE ON ME
Breathe on me, Breath of God,
Fill me with life anew,
That I may love what Thou dost love,
And do what Thou wouldst do.

Breathe on me, Breath of God,
Until my heart is pure,
Until with Thee I will one will,
To do or to endure.

Breathe on me, Breath of God,
Till I am wholly Thine;
Till all this earthly part of me
Glows with Thy fire divine.

113

Symbols of the Holy Spirit

Breathe on me, Breath of God,
So shall I never die,
But live with Thee the perfect life
Of Thine eternity.

—Edwin Hatch.

The Knowledge of the Winds

I believe that we have often misconstrued the words of Jesus, "The wind bloweth where it listeth, and thou hearest the sound thereof, but canst not tell whence it cometh, and whither it goeth." He was not stating the impossibility for man scientifically to understand the nature and characteristics of the wind. Weymouth seeks to correct this erroneous conclusion, and translates the verse as follows: "The wind bloweth where it chooses, and you hear its sound, but you do not know where it comes from or where it is going." In other words, Jesus is not denying the science of meteorology, but simply stating that in spite of any knowledge we may have, the wind still remains a riddle.

We may know the causes; we may even know the general direction of the wind; but we do not control its sovereignty, for it blows where it chooses. Man neither controls the winds of the heavens nor determines their direction, any more than he can control the breath of God or the winds of the Holy Spirit. Solomon makes this statement in the verse quoted before, and which still remains true: "Thou knowest not what is the way of the spirit" (Eccl. 11:5).

Now let us seek to discover the lessons in the comparison of what we might call a physical and spiritual meteorology, especially as the science applies to the winds. We are told that wind is simply air in motion. The scientist tells us that on account of friction at the surface of the earth, air is always in turbulent motion, eddies being formed in much the same way as in a stream of water moving over an uneven bed. The scientist has his maps on which he is able to chart the direction of the winds. The Beaufort Scale, introduced by Admiral Sir Francis Beaufort of the British Navy in 1806, is used by those making the International Weather Report. This simple scale shows the velocity of the wind. It employs the digits between 0 and 12, zero being the lowest point of the wind or an

114

absolute calm; and then the velocity or speed of the wind is shown in its increase by the comparative numbers that are used. Twelve is the highest number, and thus identifies the wind at its highest velocity, or in the words of Beaufort, "that which no canvass could withstand."

Great strides have been made in the science of meteorology as it relates to the winds; and yet upon the admission of those most familiar with it and those who make it the special study of their life, there are still many outstanding problems, so that the winds still remain more or less of an enigma or riddle. Jesus well spoke to the master of Israel, Nicodemus, and he speaks to all others who would question the supernatural without realizing the problems presented in the natural.

Just as the winds are air in motion, so we believe that in the spiritual realm the winds of God are but the Spirit of God in action. As the scientist discovers friction at the earth's surface causing air to be always in turbulent motion, so the divine science of the Word shows that the Holy Spirit is ever in motion or activity, the power and velocity of which depends on the frictions of life at the surface of its earthly plane. God's Word becomes our Beaufort Scale, by which we trace the course and the velocity of the winds. "The wind goeth toward the south, and turneth about unto the north; it whirleth about continually, and the wind returneth again according to his circuits" (Eccl. 1:6). There is a spiritual analogy between the movements of the winds in the heavens and the Spirit of God in the life of a believer.

The Power of the Winds

Those of us who live in New England and were here in the fall of 1938 do not need to be reminded of the power of the wind. Late in the afternoon of September 21 the winds had really begun to blow. I remember leaving my study at Tremont Temple and driving to my home in Newton, but giving very little concern, for the wind had often blown before but always subsided without too much damage. As we sat at the dinner table that evening, we looked out the window and saw the trees literally rocking back and forth until they were uprooted and fell across the backyard, some of them upon the house. Then we began to realize the velocity of the winds, and the danger.

Records show that at the top of Mt. Washington the wind reached a velocity of 162 miles per hour. This was rather a freak hurricane, in that it cut a clear swathe through New England from 100–125 miles in width. The morning after the hurricane my family and I drove to Cape Cod to see if our cottage had been destroyed. We did not realize the amount of damage which had been done, nor that the police were blocking off all traffic. It so happened that we were not stopped, and as we drove from Boston to the Cape Cod Canal, we saw the evidences of the storm everywhere. Houses had been destroyed, great trees blocked portions of the road, water mains had burst; summer places, cottages, and roadside stands had been lifted from their foundations and carried yards away, where they were resting all askew after the hurricane had subsided.

Strangely enough, as we crossed the Sagamore Bridge at the eastern end of the Cape Cod Canal and went on to Cape Cod itself, we discovered a clean line of demarcation between the side devastated and the country that was absolutely untouched. It was as though a great army of engineers had drawn exact lines and gone through the country, destroying everything in their path. The American Red Cross totalled the deaths at 682. The damage to property was over $500,000,000. At the Scituate (Massachusetts) Reservoir alone, three million trees were blown down. In New England and Long Island over 57,000 homes were destroyed, and 45,000 families suffered losses. We are told that a hurricane is "a whirlpool in the atmosphere," and has the greatest speed and distance of any type of storm.

Now coming to the Holy Spirit, we discover that he is "as of a rushing, mighty wind." These are the words used to describe the coming of the Spirit on the 120 disciples on the day of Pentecost. The Greek words *pnoes* and *biaias* literally mean "a violent breath." The description is a true revelation of the might and power of the Holy Spirit. "Mighty" means powerful, and that we might know of the power of the Holy Spirit, Paul prays "that ye may know what is... the exceeding greatness of his power... according to the working of his mighty power, which he wrought

The Riddle of the Winds

in Christ, when he raised him from the dead" (Eph. 1:18-20). This mighty power of the Holy Spirit defied death in the Person of Jesus Christ, broke a Roman seal, and rolled away a Roman tombstone as though it were a pebble. It is this mighty, powerful Spirit who dwells in us in all his fullness.

A further description is that the Spirit came as a "rushing wind," and the word *pharumanos* means "like the carrying power of a mighty river." In a flood, the swollen waters carry before them everything that is not securely fixed. Just so, the Holy Spirit, when he comes as a rushing wind, sweeps away all the debris of life and that which is not built upon the secure foundation of Jesus Christ. Saints are melted, consciences are quickened, feelings stirred, bitterness expelled; jealousies fade, gossiping ceases, wrongs are confessed, restitutions are made, love becomes contagious, spirits are lightened, hope is bright, zeal is fervent, prayer is real, conduct is pure, humility is apparent, temper is controlled, tolerance is in order, service is a joy and fruitful, God is glorified, and revival fires burn.

Surely we, as individual believers and the Church of Jesus Christ, need the incoming of this rushing mighty wind, that all which is not of the Lord and giving him the preeminence might be carried away. How many problems within our churches and our own individual lives would be immediately solved if the floodgates of life were to be opened to the incoming of this mighty, cleansing power!

The Four Winds of the Heavens

The Bible mentions four directional winds of the heavens, and each of these is most suggestive of the ministry or function of the Holy Spirit in the life of the believer. We will enumerate these four winds and seek to show how this comparison is true.

Many references are made in Scripture to the east wind, and in each instance it is a wind of devastation and destruction. In the dream given to Joseph, wherein he saw the seven years of plenty and the seven years of famine, the seven thin stalks were withered by a mighty east wind. "And the seven thin and ill-favored kine that came up after them are seven years; and the seven empty ears

117

blasted with the east wind shall be seven years of famine" (Genesis 41:27).

Another evidence of the devastating power, or the use of the east wind to produce a devastating power, is found in the experience or contest of Moses with Pharaoh. A great many times Pharaoh had promised and yet broken his promise; and at last Moses, by instruction from God, threatened a plague of locusts that would destroy all the crops and enter into the homes. Pharaoh deceived Moses again, and we read, "The east wind brought the locusts" to Egypt (Ex. 10:13).

It was an east wind which discomfited Jonah: "God prepared a vehement east wind; and the sun beat upon the head of Jonah, that he fainted, and wished in himself to die" (Jon. 4:8). It was also an east wind of a more northerly direction which caused the destruction of the ship upon which the Apostle Paul was traveling. The name used in the Authorized Version to describe the storm is Euroclydon, and the literal meaning is "a furious northeast wind." Those of us who live on the Atlantic seaboard know the fury of such a wind.

By analogy, we see that as the east wind devastates and destroys, so the Holy Spirit does also. Isaiah, in his prophecy of John the Baptist, is heard to say:

> The voice said, Cry. And he said, What shall I cry?
> All flesh is grass, and all the goodliness thereof is as
> the flower of the field: The grass withereth, the flower
> fadeth; because the spirit of the Lord bloweth upon it:
> surely the people is grass (Isa. 40: 6, 7).

The winds blew upon the grass and it withered, and the flower faded; but the analogy is made between the wind and the Spirit of the Lord. Grass is symbolic of the people. Who has not seen a field of corn or wheat prostrate after the devastating wind which often accompanies a thunderstorm? So self-righteousness must wither under the breath of God. Isaiah, describing that day when Jesus Christ will come to reign as King and destroy his enemies, says: "And with the breath of his lips shall he slay the wicked" (Isa. 11:4).

Not only will he do this to his enemies in the future, but I believe that by the breath of his Holy Spirit he will slay all wickedness in us. Disobedience, pride, self-righteousness, and all those things which are grieving the Spirit of God will wither away. Marsh, in his *Emblems of the Holy Spirit*, quotes Fénelon in his description of humility which is heaven-born, as he contrasts it with the spurious meekness assumed by man. This is the greatest statement I have ever read on true humility and answers many problems that have faced all of us who have longed for such humility. Listen to him, and let his words sink deep into your consciousness.

> *He who seeks not his own interest, but solely God's interest in time and eternity, he is humble. . . . Many study exterior humility, but humility which does not flow from love is spurious. The more this exterior humility stoops, the loftier it inwardly feels itself; but he who is conscious of stooping does not really feel himself to be so low that he can go no further. People who think much of their humility are very proud. . . . Many men seeking to be humble by an effort of their will, and failing in perfect resignation and self-renunciation, sin against the Divine love without which there is no humility. Fuller light would enable them to see that they are exalting themselves by that which they mean for humility; their supposed setting aside of self is self-seeking; they are puffed up with the pride of humility, and glory in the humble acts they perform. But the really humble man does not do anything of the sort; he lets himself be carried hither and thither; he is satisfied that God should do as He will with him, as the wind with the straw; and there is more real humility in accepting greatness in such a spirit than thwarting God's plans beneath a pretext of humility. He who chooses abasement rather than eleation is not necessarily humble, though he may wish to be; but he who lets himself go—up or down—heedless whether to be praised or blamed, unmindful of what is said of him, is really humble, whatever men may think, if it be because he waits solely on God's pleasure.*

119

Symbols of the Holy Spirit

I have noticed that oftentimes those who talk with greatest piety and profess the greatest humility are, nevertheless, the victims of pride, and instead of being in the center of God's will, as they continually profess to be, to the point of boasting, are shown by their lives to be otherwise. We need to guard against such fallacious thinking and wrong action. We can be kept in the center of God's will only as the Spirit of God himself keeps us there. Oh, to be truly humble in accordance with the description of humility given above! The east wind of the Spirit of God will come in devastating power to make this condition a reality. Perhaps as from a hurricane, there may be great financial loss and physical suffering; but if we are willing to pay the price he will come.

Next in the directional winds are those that come from the west. As we study the scriptural references to these, we find that they are winds of deliverance and comfort.

It was the west wind that cleared away the locusts from the land of Egypt. "The Lord turned a mighty strong west wind, which took away the locusts" (Exod. 10:19). All of us have felt the refreshing coolness upon our bodies in the midst of a hot, sultry summer night, as the west winds gently blew through our windows to bring relief. But isn't this just what the Lord promised the Holy Spirit would be in the lives of those to whom he would come? His word to the disciples was, "I will pray the Father, and he shall give you another Comforter" (John 14:16). We know that the word for comforter is "paraclete," or the One who is called alongside; and oftentimes we have felt that the Authorized Version was not too accurate in its translation. However, perhaps there is a lesson for us to learn here; that is, that the Holy Spirit is indeed the divine Comforter.

A little boy, or so he is supposed to have been (I rather imagine his identity would be hard to prove, because the story has been told from many angles, and yet is most suggestive), was asked by his mother what the preacher had spoken about that morning. He was unable to say, but said he did remember the text. When asked for this, he said it was that God has promised "to send another bed quilt." The mother, not too well versed in Scripture, wondered to what he had reference, but learned from a friend who

The Riddle of the Winds

had heard the sermon that the reference was to the promise of the Comforter. This rather ridiculous story is not so ridiculous after all, for in the youngster's naive answer there is a world of truth.

The Holy Spirit is just that, a comforter, a deliverer from the coldness of the wintry blasts of sin, temptation, heartache, and suffering. He alone can comfort us and cover us with the warmth of the love of the Son of God. Surely all of us would desire these west winds of the Spirit, to bring comfort in the sultry, weary hours of a restless day or night.

The north wind brings clearing. "Fair weather cometh out of the north" (Job 37:22), and "The north wind driveth away rain" (Prov. 25:23). Some of the most beautiful days, with cloudless sky, follow rain, fog, and cloud when the north wind has driven them away to some other place. To me, Job makes a very significant statement when he says, "He stretcheth out the north over the empty place, and hangeth the earth upon nothing" (Job 26:7). This is a reference to the vast expanse or empty place in the north portion of the heavens.

Astronomers tell us that this is literally true. In the fourteenth chapter of Isaiah we have a partial history of Satan and the record of his attempt to usurp the place of God. He is described as Lucifer, the one who would ascend into heaven, and is quoted as saying: "I will exalt my throne above the stars of God: I will sit also upon the mount of the congregation, in the sides of the north: I will ascend above the heights of the clouds; I will be like the Most High" (Isa. 14:13, 14). Is not this reference to the north most suggestive of the fact that God dwells in the north places? Perhaps a use of our spiritual imagination might be justified when we think that the north winds come from out of the empty places immediately from the presence of God, and thus are used to clear away the rain and the clouds.

Clear spiritual weather comes to the believer by the Holy Spirit as he comes directly from the presence of God. Thus we could describe it as the north wind of the Spirit. Peter declares in his great sermon, "Repent ye therefore, and be converted, that your sins may be blotted out, when the times of refreshing shall come from the presence of the Lord" (Acts 3:19). Weymouth translates it, "that there may come seasons of refreshment from the Lord."

Symbols of the Holy Spirit

If we would have the north winds of the Spirit bringing clear, refreshing weather, bright skies, and plenteous grace into our life, then there must be no barriers between us and him; for these times of refreshment must come directly from his presence.

> *God hath not promised skies always blue,*
> *Flower-strewn pathways all our lives through;*
> *God hath not promised sun without rain,*
> *Joy without sorrow, peace without pain.*
>
> *But God hath promised strength for the day,*
> *Rest for the labor, light on the way;*
> *Grace for the trial, help from above,*
> *Unfailing sympathy, undying love.*
>
> —Annie Johnson Flint.

The last of the four winds reveals perhaps the most precious ministry of the Spirit. The south winds are those of pleasantness and delight. Solomon says: "Awake, O north wind; and come, thou south; blow upon my garden, that the spices thereof may flow out" (Song 4:16). As these words are being written, I look out the window on a beautiful, sunny winter sky, and though it is warm on the inside, it is cold just outside my window. I long for the coming of the summer, so the southerly winds can sweep across the narrow strip of land called Cape Cod and fill the sails of my sailboat to take me and my family over the blue waters in one of the most delightful recreations I know. The south wind means summer warmth, growing gardens, beautiful flowers, increased pleasure, sun-tanned bodies, a vacation season, and enjoyments for all. This is the playtime of the year.

But there is also the playtime and the loveliness of the Spirit's influence on our life. The Holy Spirit will come like the gentle south winds, blowing across our life to bring the warmth of summer, the garden of flowers, reproducing in us the lily of the valley and the rose of Sharon, and the very savor of his love. We will be refreshed and quickened in body, mind, and soul; spiritual and physical health will be given; and the beauty of the Lord our God will be upon us. Frances Ridley Havergal, in a poem, "The Message of the AEolian Harp," tells of her futile attempt to play a

122

The Riddle of the Winds

harp given to her, and of discovering the secret. It is given in the course of a conversation between one Eleanor and Beatrice, and it is most suggestive.

> *A friend, a kind, dear friend*
> *Gave me this harp, that should be all my own,*
> *That it might speak to me in twilight lone*
> *When other sounds were fled; that it might send*
> *Sweet messages of calming, cheering might,*
> *Sweet sudden thrills of strange and exquisite delight.*

But the harp gave forth no music as she tried to play it, and she learned that she must place it where the cool breezes might play upon it.

> *I waited till the sun had set,*
> *And twilight fell upon the autumn sea;*
> *I watched, and saw the south wind touch a tree,*
> *Dark outlined on the paling gold, and yet*
> *My harp was mute. I cried, "Awake, O south!*
> *Come to my harp, and call its answering music forth!"*

Then first one low sweet note was heard, a promise of what would follow: strange vibrations rising and falling, quivering silver chords. Then silence, and suddenly the harp playing a march for an angelic host:

> *Thus, while the holy stars did shine*
> *And listen, these aeolian marvels breathed;*
> *While love and peace and gratitude enwreathed*
> *With rich delight in one fair crown were mine.*
> *The wind that bloweth where it listeth brought*
> *This glory of harp-music,—not my skill or thought.*
>
> *She ceased. Then Eleanor looked up,*
> *And said, "O Beatrice, I too have tried*
> *My finger-skill in vain. But opening now*
> *My window, like wise Daniel, I will set*
> *My little harp therein, and listening wait*
> *The breath of heaven, the Spirit of our God."*

I have taken the liberty of changing to south the direction of the wind which she identified as north. The north wind would bring melody from the harp, but because of its force perhaps not so beautifully as the south winds, which are more gentle. O that we might be wise and place the aeolian harp of our life in the open window, that the southerly winds of the divine Spirit himself might bring forth music all his own! Life can be filled with beauty and with music, but only as the Spirit plays the strings of the harp of life.

Thus we have seen the spiritual analogy between the winds of heaven and the Spirit of God, sometimes called the Breath of God. In the riddle of the winds we discover again the paramount message of Jesus, "Ye must be born again" (John 3:7). This statement of Jesus, and the necessity of the new birth, should not be questioned; for only through the new birth, the birth of the spirit, can the Holy Spirit be given to us and come into the experience of life like the winds of heaven come upon the earth. To those who have been born again, but who have become very much like the dry bones in the valley of Ezekiel's vision, the reviving of the Spirit of God may come as the Spirit himself falls fresh on each of us. Hear again the prophecy of Ezekiel, and with it the recording of the results, in an exceeding great army:

> *Prophesy unto the wind, prophesy, son of man, and say to the wind, Thus saith the Lord God: Come from the four winds, O breath, and breathe upon these slain, that they may live. So I prophesied as he commanded me, and the breath came into them, and they lived and stood up upon their feet, an exceeding great army* (Ezek. 37:9, 10).

This day of armies, with many million men serving in the armed forces of the United States, needs to find a counterpart in the exceeding great army of the Lord. Let our prayer be that the Spirit of God shall breathe fresh upon us, bringing to us the four winds from the east, the west, the north, and the south, either to devastate and destroy, as the need may be, or to deliver, bring fair weather and clear skies, and then the loveliness of the life superbly beautiful, made possible through the southerly winds of God's Spirit.

OIL FOR THE LIGHT   10
THAT LIGHTS THE WORLD

"Ye are the light of the world. A city that is set on an hill cannot be hid." (Matthew 5:14)

From earliest times man has endeavored to produce artificial light, that he might utilize more throughly the hours of darkness for work or pleasure. Until the first application of electricity to lighting late in the nineteenth century, all artificial light was produced by fire. The first means of securing light at night was the wood fire, and in order to light the way a burning stick called a firebrand or torch was picked from the fire and carried by the individual. From that primitive method until the present day great progress has been made, but more especially during the last century and a half. One might, in line with similar terminology in other fields, properly describe the present as a light age. Today's lighting is comparatively inexpensive and health-producing, in that it saves overstrained and tired eyes.

It is interesting to follow the development of light. We discover that oil lamps had their origin several thousand years before Christ. The prehistoric oil lamp was probably made of stone, then clay, and afterward of terra-cotta. These lamps had one wick and a reservoir of oil or grease to saturate the wick, making possible the flame. Later there came the wax candle, which was probably of Phoenician origin; and then the tallow candle, first used in the second century after Christ. The two most modern means of lighting are gas and electricity. Gas was first used for this purpose by

125

the Chinese. They piped natural gas through bamboo tubes from the salt mines and used it to give illumination.

It fell to a British preacher, the Rev. Dr. John Clayton of Wigand, Lancashire, England, to start the real revolution of artificial illuminating gas. About 1664 he drained water from a ditch under which was a natural gas well and discovered the gas coming from the ground. A coal mine was near by, and he suspected a relationship. He distilled the coal in a retort and succeeded in collecting some of the coal gas. In 1784, more than a century later, Jean Pierre Minckelers, then professor at Louvain University, distilled many substances, including coal, and in 1785 lighted his classroom with gas. From then on, developments began to increase until, in our present day, gas used for illumination is as nearly perfect as science can make it.

Of course, we are best acquainted with electricity. In 1752 Benjamin Franklin, experimenting with a Leyden jar, discovered the secret of lightning—natural electricity. Fifty years later Sir Humphrey Davy demonstrated the practicability of obtaining electricity from cells consisting of unlike metals immersed in an acid solution. The name of Thomas A. Edison is the most familiar of all. His basic lamp patent, No. 223898, has been upheld by the courts as covering the modern incandescent lamps. Those who have read the story of Edison know of the remarkable work done by this twentieth-century genius.

By 1928 over one million electric lamps were sold. We have no figures for the next decade, but, with the increase of construction and light improvement, we would not wonder if this amount was doubled or trebled. In fact, the progress has been so great that we accept the benefits with little interest in the question as to how they have been made possible.

But we are not concerned with artificial lighting, for we are considering the subject, "Oil for the Light that Lights the World." And this of course is a reference to the statement of Jesus, "Ye are the light of the world" (Matt. 5:14), and the supply of the Holy Spirit as oil for the lighting of our spiritual lamps. Therefore, let us consider together a comparison of artificial with spiritual lighting, for there is a direct spiritual counterpart or history. The Word says: "In him was life; and the life was the light

Oil for the Light That Lights the World

of men. And the light shineth in darkness; and the darkness comprehended it not" (John 1:4, 5). Here is the key that unlocks the door to the laboratory where we learn the science of spiritual lighting, without which no man can see God.

The Holy Spirit is the oil or source by which this light has always burned. Remember that artificial light is produced by some power within the lamp. It was first by fire, then by the use of a wick saturated with oil, then with a wick placed in wax or tallow called a candle; after that gas, and, finally, electricity conveyed to a filament of highly resistant carbon through platinum wires in a vacuum, made possible by a chamber composed entirely of glass, and closed at all points by the fusion thereof. In the spiritual counterpart we find that spiritual light is produced by divine energy in the person of the Holy Spirit, present in the vacuum chamber or the life of the believer, producing the light of Christ on the filament of transformed human personality. Thus from the laboratory of physical science and spiritual revelation we continue our study of oil for the light that lights the world.

The History of Spiritual Lighting

One who would know the history of things spiritual must discover it in the Word of God, finding it in its beginnings and following it through the entire Word. The words of John, "In him was life; and the life was the light of men" (John 1:4), send us back to the beginning of the Word. Jesus Christ was and is the Light Eternal. He is "the image of the invisible God" (Col. 1:15), and he is also "the brightness of his glory, and the express image of his person" (Heb. 1:3). Paul says, "For God, who commanded the light to shine out of darkness, hath shined in our hearts, to give the light of the knowledge of the glory of God in the face of Jesus Christ" (2 Cor. 4:6). Thus, when we hear Jesus making the claim, "I am the light of the world" (John 8:12), we know that it is corroborated by the witness of the entire Word.

In the beginning of creation he became the life and the light of men. Adam, the first of all creation, received this life and light in Christ, but almost immediately reached out and extinguished the light by his own volition. In regeneration the light was put on

127

again, as we shall later see. That which had been extinguished by sin has been relighted by the Son of man.

In order that we may have a proper understanding of the Spirit's ministry in this realm of spiritual light, it is necessary that we discover the Light Prophetic, or National Light. God chose Israel, the seed of Abraham, to be a nation in which he might dwell and through which he might reveal himself to the other nations of the world. When God gave Moses the instructions for building and equipping the Tabernacle, he provided for the seven-branched candlestick: "Thou shalt make a candlestick of pure gold. . . . Six branches shall come out of the sides of it; three branches of the candlestick out of the one side, and three branches of the candlestick out of the other side" (Exod. 25:31, 32). We believe that this seven-branched candlestick is symbolic of Israel's national or prophetic witness.

God had said to Abraham: "I will bless thee, and make thy name great; and thou shalt be a blessing . . . and in thee shall all the families of the earth be blessed" (Gen. 12:2, 3).. This was not only a prophecy in regard to Jesus Christ, the seed of Abraham, but also a prophecy of the place and ministry of Israel in the world. That Israel has a prophetic witness or light-giving ministry is the testimony of Isaiah: "I will also give thee for a light to the Gentiles" (Isa. 49:6). Sadly, the light did not burn for long or with great clearness; for soon, through idolatry and rejection, captivity and isolation, Israel caused her light to be extinguished. Some of us believe that the light will yet burn for the great national and prophetic witness of this ancient people. Surely it is not burning in our own day, but God's decrees and plans are not set aside by the action and whim of man.

For our greater interest, we come to what might be called the unique light of the believer; and it is this light to which we refer in the subject of our message and to which Jesus refers in our text. As we turn to the New Testament and to the first chapter of the Book of Revelation, we discover that there are seven golden candlesticks in contrast with the seven-branched candlestick of the Old Testament: "I saw seven golden candlesticks; and in the midst of the seven candlesticks one like unto the Son of man" (Rev. 1:12, 13). Notice, there are no longer seven branches but only one branch, seven candlesticks, each one individual and each one bearing its own light. This we believe to be a symbol of the individual witness of the believer.

Jesus said, "Ye are the light of the world" (Matt. 5:14), and as a golden candlestick each of us has become a light. He also said, "I am the light of the world" (John 8:12), and thus he is revealing his own divine light in and through the individual believer. Some might say that the seven candlesticks refer to the seven churches, with the Son of man in the midst. But the seven churches must make reference to all, the complete body of Christ, as well as to the seven churches in Asia Minor; and the complete body of Christ is simply the sum total of all individuals who through the new birth and baptism in the Spirit have been made part of that body. The gospel is always individual first and social afterward. Individual believers are a spiritual light that makes possible the spiritual lighting of this dark world.

The Oil That Flows to the Lamps of Christians

In order properly to evaluate and understand the ministry of the Holy Spirit as the source of oil from which the lamps of believers are lighted, it will be necessary to review the ministry of the Holy Spirit in the Old Testament. In the vision of Zerubbabel as recorded by Zechariah, we read:

> *What seest thou? And I said, I have looked, and behold a candlestick all of gold . . . and his seven lamps thereon, and seven pipes to the seven lamps, which are upon the top thereof: and two olive trees by it, one upon the right side of the bowl, and the other upon the left side thereof. . . . What be these two olive branches, which through the two golden pipes empty the golden oil out of themselves?* (Zech. 4:2, 3, 12).

Here is the statement of a vision, and then the question as to the meaning thereof. It is clear that the reference is to the Holy Spirit, for we read: "This is the word of the Lord unto Zerubbabel, saying, Not by might nor by power, but by my Spirit, saith the Lord of hosts" (Zech. 4:6). In the vision, the two olive branches are connected with the two golden pipes, and these to the seven lamps. The oil flowed from the olive branches into the golden pipes, and through these to the reservoirs of the seven candlesticks. Thus the oil would flow with undiminishing supply. But the Word of the Lord to Zerubbabel was that it was not by physical power, or even by the oil of the olive, but "by my Spirit, saith the Lord of hosts." Thus the oil in the Old Testament directly refers to the Holy Spirit.

Coming now to the ministry of the Holy Spirit as the oil supplied to light the lamps of Christians, we study the relationship of the Holy Spirit to the believer in this dispensation. First, we must recognize that the Holy Spirit is now given individually, and not nationally as he was to the nation Israel. We should also determine that he is given permanently as the eternal life, and not transiently and for certain purposes as to individuals of the Old Testament era. It would be well to let Paul speak here.

> *Now there are diversities of gifts, but the same Spirit. And there are differences of administrations, but the same Lord. And there are diversities of operations, but it is the same God which worketh all in all. But the manifestation of the Spirit is given to every man to profit withal. For to one is given by the Spirit the word of wisdom; to another the word of knowledge by the same Spirit; to another faith by the same Spirit; to another the gifts of healing by the same Spirit; to another the working of miracles; to another prophecy; to another discerning of spirits; to another divers kinds of tongues; to another the interpretation of tongues: but all these worketh that one and the selfsame Spirit, dividing to every man severally as he will* (1 Cor. 12:4-11).

Thus we see that to each individual the Holy Spirit has been given, and even though there may be different gifts, all of these work for the selfsame purpose, the glory of God. Reading the story of Pentecost, we discover that "there appeared unto them cloven tongues like as of fire, and it sat upon *each* of them" (Acts 2:3). Remember that in the first chapter of Revelation we saw the seven

Oil for the Light That Lights the World

individual candlesticks and the Son of man in the midst. Thus in these two instances we find the verification of the fact that the Spirit is given individually. At Pentecost he sat upon each, and in the vision of the Apocalypse the Son of man was in the midst of the seven individual candlesticks.

Here is the difference dispensationally between the Old and the New Testament ministries of the Spirit. In the Old Testament his ministry was, first, national and second, individual, but for specific purposes only. This is shown in the case of the prophets, in the life of Samson as the Spirit of God came upon him and gave needed strength, and especially in the case of Bezaleel: "And Moses said unto the children of Israel, See, the Lord hath called by name Bezaleel the son of Uri, the son of Hur, of the tribe of Judah; and he hath filled him with the spirit of God, in wisdom, in understanding, and in knowledge, and in all manner of workmanship" (Exod. 35:30, 31). This was so that Bezaleel might do the work of a craftsman, necessary in the carrying out of the pattern and program of God.

Peter tells us that the prophets were holy men upon whom the Holy Spirit came. He exercised his divine purpose in and through them, and when this purpose was accomplished, withdrew. Of course, there should always be this clear fact in mind, that in all ages the Spirit is not only the author but the life itself of the believer.

As intimated before, the Holy Spirit gives a full and undiminishing supply. "God giveth not the Spirit by measure" (John 3:34). Or as Weymouth translates this verse, "God does not give the Spirit in sparing measure." Just now, during these winter months, we have a shortage of coal for heating homes. Thank God, there is no shortage in the supply of the Holy Spirit when once the conversion is made and the soul is turned from Satan to God, from sin to righteousness.

Light Rays of the Oil of the Holy Spirit

Now we shall seek to determine the ministry of the Holy Spirit as the light ray in the revelation of God through all ages. The Holy Spirit was symbolized in the perpetual flame found in the Taber-

131

nacle. "Thou shalt command the children of Israel, that they bring thee pure oil olive beaten for the light, to cause the lamp to burn always. In the tabernacle of the congregation without the veil, which is before the testimony . . ." (Exod. 27:20, 21). Here was the lamp which burned continually, fed by the pure olive oil, and symbolizing the presence of God in the midst of the Tabernacle. This light burned without the veil, which was before the testimony. "Without the veil" means the place from which Moses and Aaron spoke to the people. It was outside the holiest place of all, which was found within the inner veil. This was the place of the testimony, the ark of the covenant, the mercy seat; and this place was forbidden to all except Aaron the high priest, and was admissible to him but once a year, when he came in his priestly office to make atonement for the people.

Thus the light burned, not in this holiest place of all, but in the holy place, between the first and second veils. This was the place of the shewbread, the pot of incense, and the light which burned from the golden candlestick. It corresponds in type to the believer's body, in which the eternal flame of the Holy Spirit burns. Paul said to the Corinthians: "What! know ye not that your body is the temple of the Holy Ghost which is in you, which ye have of God . . . ?" (1 Cor. 6:19). There are two words used in the New Testament that are interpreted "temple." One of these is *heiron*. It is used by John in the eighth chapter when he tells us: "Jesus went unto the mount of Olives. And early in the morning he came again into the temple, and all the people came unto him; and he sat down, and taught them" (John 8:1, 2). This is a direct reference to the Temple area, into which all the people could come, and not to the holy place within the Temple.

The other word is the Greek word *naos*; and this word, according to Thayer, is used of the Temple at Jerusalem, but only of the sacred sanctuary itself, consisting of the holy place and the holy of holies. Thus we see that the perpetual light in the seven-branched golden candlestick that was in the holy place of the Tabernacle is a direct type of the perpetual and eternal flame of the Holy Spirit in the life of the believer, which has become God's holy place or tabernacle upon earth. The Holy Spirit, according to Jesus' testimony, is here to bear witness to him.

Oil for the Light That Lights the World

Jesus said, "I am the light of the world." And of us, "Ye are the light of the world." Thus we see that his light in us is made possible by the eternal indwelling and fire of the Holy Spirit.

The Holy Spirit has become for the believer a guiding light in a heavenly fellowship. In his first epistle John says:

> *God is light, and in him is no darkness at all. If we say that we have fellowship with him, and walk in darkness, we lie, and do not the truth: but if we walk in the light, as he is in the light, we have fellowship one with another, and the blood of Jesus Christ his Son cleanseth us from all sin. . . . Truly our fellowship is with the Father, and with his Son, Jesus Christ* (1 John 1:5-7, 3).

There can be no darkness in this heavenly fellowship, and darkness can be dispelled only by the light of the Holy Spirit, who reveals to us the light of Christ, or the light of God, in whom there is no darkness at all. Thus we see that by the indwelling of the Holy Spirit there is the possibility of a lighted pathway for the believer in this earthly yet heavenly fellowship. This is made possible first of all through the Spirit's indwelling. Paul says, "If we live in the Spirit, let us also walk in the Spirit" (Gal. 5:25). God gave Israel a pillar of cloud by day and a pillar of fire by night, symbolical of the presence of the indwelling Holy Spirit, in order that he might lead us by day and night.

> *Holy Spirit, faithful Guide,*
> *Ever near the Christian's side;*
> *Gently lead us by the hand,*
> *Pilgrims in a desert land;*
> *Weary souls fore'er rejoice,*
> *While they hear that sweetest voice,*
> *Whisp'ring softly, "Wand'rer, come!*
> *Follow me, I'll guide thee home."*
>
> *Ever present, truest Friend,*
> *Ever near thine aid to lend,*
> *Leave us not to doubt and fear,*
> *Groping on in darkness drear;*

Symbols of the Holy Spirit

When the storms are raging sore,
Hearts grow faint, and hopes give o'er;
Whisper softly, "Wand'rer, come!
Follow me, I'll guide thee home."

Secondly, he becomes the guiding light of this earthly yet heavenly fellowship through his Word. The Psalmist said, "Thy word is a lamp unto my feet, and a light unto my path" (Psa. 119:105). The Word is the instrument of the Holy Spirit; but it is also the lamp of God. And thus in the Word we find the Holy Spirit, through his teaching, illuminating our pathway. It has indeed become a lamp unto our feet and a light unto our path. We are told that in olden days the miner had a light on the toe of one of his boots to illuminate his path. Blessed be the Christian whose pathway is lighted by the light that shines from the Word of God!

Jesus said, "Let your light so shine before men, that they may see your good works, and glorify your Father which is in heaven" (Matt. 5:16). This is the burning light that is ours in the flame of his purity. On the Mount of Transfiguration "his raiment was white as the light" (Matt. 17:2). This was made possible by the full indwelling of the Holy Spirit, for it was the light of his purity and absolute sinlessness. And we know that that sinlessness was given by the full indwelling of the Spirit of God, for Christ "through the eternal Spirit offered himself without spot to God" (Heb. 9:14). But the same Spirit dwells in us, by the same ministry producing in us this transfiguration purity. True, we cannot have that transfiguration glory now, because we are still earthly, still having a carnal nature. And yet when the golden pipes are clear channels, and the bowl is filled with the oil of the Spirit, the lamp all trimmed and the chimney clean, then the light must shine.

There is a further blessing in the indwelling flame of the Holy Spirit, as suggested to us in the parable of the virgins. It is the flame that gives justifiable composure in a world of darkness. There were five wise and five foolish virgins; but of the wise it is said, "The wise took oil in their vessels with their lamps. While the bridegroom tarried, they all slumbered and slept" (Matt. 25:4, 5). These were justified in their composure, for they had prepared against the day of the bridegroom's coming. In other words, they possessed oil, and were not merely pretenders carrying lamps without oil. To them the coming of the bridegroom gave no sense of fear. They were not restless or fretful in their waiting, but possessed a patience born of the knowledge that oil was in the lamps.

This is the patience that is born of the Spirit of God. "For we through the Spirit wait for the hope of righteousness by faith" (Gal. 5:5). Paul said to the believers at Thessalonica: "For our gospel came not unto you in word only, but also in power, and in the Holy Ghost, and in much assurance.... And ye became followers of us, and of the Lord, having received the word in much affliction, with joy in the Holy Ghost... so that ye were ensamples to all that believe.... ye turned to God from idols to serve the living and true God; and to wait for his Son from heaven" (1 Thess. 1:5, 6, 9, 10). Only those who have the lamp of life filled with the oil of the Holy Spirit and the perpetual flame of the Spirit dwelling within can face the future with composure and confidence and be among those whom Paul describes as able "to wait for his Son from heaven." Many people know all about the return of Christ, but have never found composure in this blessed waiting. Only those can have this composure who have recognized that through being born again they have become the recipients of God the Holy Spirit.

In the world of tomorrow artificial lighting will indeed produce the physical fulfillment of a spiritual prophecy, "Thy darkness shall be as the noonday" (Isa. 58:10). By the hand of science the darkness of tomorrow will be illuminated. We will live in an age of artificial light. But even though the darkness may be as noonday, the light producing it will never be sufficient to give spiritual illumination that will enlighten the moral and sinful darkness in which our world has been enshrouded. Jesus said, "Ye are the light of the world."

Remember, each believer is as the individual candlestick, and the light must shine through us; for we individually are the lights that light the world. Collectively, the Church which is the body of Jesus Christ is the light that lights the world. Would it be irreverent to say that the Lamplighter stands in the midst? For in the vision of John on Patmos we see "in the midst... one like unto the Son of man" (Rev. 1:13). He it is who has made possible the

135

Symbols of the Holy Spirit

supply of the Spirit. He it is who relights the extinguished flame of our unregenerate life, by the divine touch of Calvary. Thus the light that was extinguished may be lit again.

In modern lighting, electricity is conveyed through platinum wires to a filament of highly resistant carbon, both in a vacuum made possible by exhausting a chamber made entirely of glass and fused together at all points. But to make illumination possible, energy must be brought in from the outside, through the platinum wires. As the power is conveyed from the great power plants to give light to the world, just so the oil of the Holy Spirit is the divine energy present in the vacuum chamber or life of the believer to produce the light of Christ on the filament of transformed human personality. The power is conveyed from that objective relationship in him which we call salvation or regeneration.

Once again, let us hear the words of Jesus as he uses this figure of speech to teach us that we are redeemed, lights that alone can lighten the world in its darkness. "Ye are the light of the world. . . . Let your light so shine before men, that they may see your good works and glorify your Father which is in heaven" (Matt. 5:14, 16).

His lamp am I, to shine where He shall say,
And lamps are not for sunny rooms,
Nor for the light of day;
But for dark places of the earth,
Where shame and crime and wrong have birth;
Or for the murky twilight gray,
Where wandering sheep have gone astray;
Or where the light of faith grows dim
And souls are groping after Him.

And as sometimes a flame we find,
Clear, shining through the night,
So bright we do not see the lamp,
But only see the light;
So I may shine—His light the flame—
That men may glorify His name.

—Annie Johnson Flint.

136

CONCLUSION

Diversity in life is always a blessing. Blessed is the preacher who realizes that the Word of God contains many kinds of truth, and thus does not become a hobbyist or preacher of any single doctrine to the exclusion of the others. There are many more figures of speech in the Word of God that could be employed and studied with great interest and untold blessing. However, for this writer, the Spirit of God now seems to lead into the searching for and preaching of other doctrines contained in the Book. Therefore, we bring our study to its conclusion for a time. But sometime we will take it up again, to discover new treasures from the mine of God's eternal truth.

I hope that those who have studied the foregoing chapters may desire to continue further than time or space now permit. A proper understanding of the Spirit's ministry is absolutely essential to him who would enjoy the full measure of God's blessing and wield a real influence among his fellowmen. In other words, wrong interpretations of the ministry of the Holy Spirit result in confusion and cause the Christian to do things which have no justification in the admonition of the Word nor in the example revealed in the life of Christ. Sane-thinking, cultured people turn away in disgust.

But when a wholesome, beautiful, serene, and sane life is revealed through the knowledge of the Spirit's ministry within, then people who believe that life can be beautiful and who desire to use the mind that God has given them and to think and act in a way that is harmonious with the very best things of life will seek

the way and secret of such a life. Oh, that we might have his likeness upon us at all times! For he was indeed "altogether lovely"
(Song 5:16). I believe that this is the purpose of the Holy Spirit in
his ministry to each believer, that this loveliness of the "altogether
lovely" Lord Jesus Christ might be ours.

Many thoughts and suggestions set forth in the foregoing chapters have come through wide reading and help received from those
to whom the Spirit has spoken, and who in turn have recorded
their thoughts. The scientific analogies or comparisons are the
result of individual research in textbooks and other sources; and
the author's indebtedness to learned men in every realm of science
is gladly acknowledged. Oh, that many of these scientists might
have the deeper knowledge of the revelation of God's Spirit, that
they might see themselves in their scientific discoveries as but the
instruments used by God to confirm his great eternal decrees, and,
above all, his great plan of redemption, not only for man, but for
creation itself! No man can see the hand of God in creation and be
without excuse in his foolhardiness of denial and rejection. It was
the Psalmist who said: "The fool hath said in his heart, There is
no God" (Psa. 14:1). It was the learned Apostle who said:

> For the wrath of God is revealed from heaven against
> all ungodliness and unrighteousness of men, who hold
> the truth in unrighteousness; because that which may
> be known of God is manifest in them; for God hath
> showed it unto them. For the invisible things of him
> from the creation of the world are clearly seen, being
> understood by the things that are made, even his eter-
> nal power and Godhead; so that they are without
> excuse. . . . Professing themselves to be wise, they be-
> came fools. . . . Wherefore God also gave them up . . .
> who changed the truth of God into a lie, and wor-
> shipped and served the creature more than the Cre-
> ator, who is blessed for ever. Amen (Romans 1:18-25).

These are among the strongest words that have ever been
uttered, and they are a blanket indictment of all those of scientific
mind and wide knowledge who yet reject the revelation of God.

To those of great mind and to those of lesser understanding

Conclusion

who have found the joy of a redeemed life and a teaching far above the power of human instruction, through the indwelling and revelation of the divine Spirit, there come a knowledge and a joy that surpass all wisdom and relate man to his God through Jesus Christ, God's only Son. My prayer is that these messages will edify and instruct them, strengthen and give them courage; and, above all, that they may be the divine impetus for more consecrated and holy living, that in all things Christ may have the preeminence.